GRIDIRON GLADIATORS

GRIDIRON GLADIATORS

Italian-Americans
in
College, Semipro & Pro Football

Vol. I
20s–30s–40s

Fausto Batella

iUniverse, Inc.
New York Lincoln Shanghai

GRIDIRON GLADIATORS

Italian-Americans in College, Semipro & Pro Football

iUniverse books may be ordered through booksellers or by contacting:

iUniverse
2021 Pine Lake Road, Suite 100
Lincoln, NE 68512
www.iuniverse.com
1-800-Authors (1-800-288-4677)

ISBN: 978-0-595-47827-9 (pbk)
ISBN: 978-0-595-60036-6 (ebk)

Printed in the United States of America

Contents

AKNOWLEDGMENTS

Even though I live in a small town of Central Italy, in the last 25 years I had the luck to receive and read the necessary magazine «The Coffin Corner» and a lot of books about football (most often second-hand copies) that were very important to me: thanks to them I discovered and later grasped the essence of the sport of my life.
Here you will find a list of these books, catalogued by year of printing:

1964

Bill Dudley & Robert Smith
HOW THE PROS PLAY FOOTBALL (Doubleday)

1969

Howard Liss
AFL DREAM BACKFIELD (Cowles Book Company)

1972

Fred Merrick
DOWN ON THE FARM A Story of Stanford Football (The Strode Publishers)

1975

Ken Rappoport
The Syracuse Football Story (The Strode Publishers)

1977

Weeb Ewbank, Jack Buck, Bob Broeg
FOOTBALL GREATS (The Bethany Press)

Jay Dunn
THE TIGERS OF PRINCETON Old Nassau Football (The Strode Publishers)

1979

Bert Randolh Sugar
The SEC A Pictorial History of Southeastern Conference Football (Bobbs-Merrill)

1982

John Sullivan
THE BIG GAME
California vs Stanford (Leisure Press)

Chuck Brigth
UNIVERSITY OF IOWA FOOTBALL
The Hawkeyes (Strode Publishers)

1984

Robert Our
COLLEGE FOOTBALL ALMANAC (Barnes&Noble)

Mike Rathet, Don R. Smith
The Pro Football Hall of Fame present:
Their Deeds and Dogged Faith (Rutledge Books)

1985

Richard Whittingham
SATURDAY AFTERNOON
College football and the men who made the day (Workman Publishing)

1986

Beau Riffenburgh
The Official NFL Encyclopedia (NAL books)

Carlton Stowers
Cotton Bowl Classic, The First Fifty Years (Host Communication)

1987

David Neft & Richard Cohen (with Robert Carroll and John Hogrogian)
Pro Football:THE EARLY YEARS An Encyclpedic History, 1892–1959 (Sports Products)

GREY CUP TRADITION (Executive Sport Publications/CFL) [Official Commemorative Book]

David Porter
Biographical Dictionary of American Sports: FOOTBALL (Greenwood Press)

1988

John Bowman
IVY LEAGUE FOOTBALL (Crescent Books))

Roland Lazenby
NOTRE DAME FOOTBALL (Crescent Books)

1989

Bob Gill and Tod Maher
THE OUTSIDERS
The Three American Football Leagues of 1936–41 (P.F.R.A.)

1990

Bob Gill
A MINOR MASTERPIECE
Vol. I: The American Association, 1936–41 (P.F.R.A.)

A MINOR MASTERPIECE
Vol.II:The American Football League, 1946–1950 (P.F.R.A.)

1991

James Whalen, Sr.
GRIDIRON GREATS NOW GONE
The Heyday of 19 Former Consensus Top-20 College Football Programs (McFarland)

1995

THE HEISMAN
Sixty Years of Tradition and Excellence (Adventure Quest, Inc.)

Jeannie Morris
BRIAN PICCOLO A short season (Bonus Books Inc.)

1997

Bob Carroll, Michael Gersham, David Neft, John Thorn
TOTAL FOOTBALL
The Official Encyclopedia of NFL (HarperCollins)

2001

Keith Marder, Mark Spellen, Jim Donovan
NOTRE DAME FOOTBALL ENCYCLOPEDIA
The Ultimate Guide to America's Favorite College Team (Citadel Press)

A special word of thanks to Fabiano Massimi for help with translation.
The helmet on the cover belongs to *Gladiatori Roma,* the first football team founded in Italy.

Fausto Batella
October 15, 2007

THE EARLY YEARS

Before the Twenties, only a few Italian-American athletes left quality marks in the history of college football or among the first semi-pro steps of the sport.

Ed «Batty» Abbaticchio, born in the February of 1877, is in 1895 the fullback and kicker of Latrobe (PA), the first professional gridiron team in the nation. Coach Fielding Yost credits him for the inventing of the *Spiral punt*. Two years later he signs a contract with the Philadelphia Athletics «hit and run» team. He will play in the Majors until 1910

Giovanni R. Villa is the tackle of the Michigan University team in 1895 and 1896; the same player is assistant-coach in 1898, when Michigan wins all the games disputed and conquers the conference title.

From 1901 to 1905 **Ray Abbaticchio** plays for Georgetown University; **John Bariscello** follows him in the same from 1909 to 1911.

Between 1908 and 1912 **Vincent «Pat» Pazzetti** is the team-captain, All-America quarterback on 1912 Lehigh, a team that goes 9–2–0. He also serves as the team's punter and place-kicker; and as a member of the baseball team (as a pitcher). Pat will be inducted posthumously to the National Football Foundation Sports Hall of Fame in 1961.

In the years 1910–1913, in Georgetown, **Harry Costello** excels as a ball carrier, a passer and a punter.

In 1915 **Neno «Jerry» DaPrato** is the first player of Michigan State ever to be nominated *All-American*.

In 1914–15, Tulane University hosts a leading player whose surname is **Alderatti** (coming from a family of medicians).

In 1919 **Rube Ursella** from Rock Island is the best scorer in the Ohio League; **Sammy Ciminella**, a guard, plays in the Youngstown Patricians. In the same 1919, some «paisà» (**Maio, Pace, Gardello**) get into the spotlight in the East Coast semi-pro leagues developed around the big shipyards born from World War I.

THE TWENTIES

BACKDROP

In 1920 the APFA (*American Professional Football Association*) organizes the first pro-football tournament; famed Jim «Bright Path» Thorpe is the president of the Association, more on behalf of his talents than of his amministrative and organizative abilities.

In 1922 the Association changes its name to *National Football League*; Joe Carr is the new commissioner; «**Hank**» **Gillo** is the leading scorer of the league.

In 1925 sport promoter **Pete Laudati** builds one of the first football domes, the 10,000 seats Providence Cyclodome.

Also in 1925 San Francisco hosts the first edition of the *East-West Shrine Game*; the two teams involved are composed from a selection of college all-stars. The first emigrated athlete, «**Scanlon**» **Santone** from Campobasso, Italy, debuts in the NFL. In the same year **Fred DeStefano** is in the roster of the NFL champion team.

In 1926 is born another football tradition: the appearing and quick disappearing of a competing league to NFL. The first challenger is AFL (*American Football League*), which will play only one season gathering 9 teams in major cities. Finally it will come to a compromise, obtaining some franchises from NFL. One of the winners of the first and only AFL titles, there is also a «**Butch**» **Spagna**.

Also in 1926, the University of Wisconsin instals the first electro-mechanical scoreboard. The machine makes its debut during the game against Iowa.

In 1927 the dead calm returns; NFL puts 2 teams in New York, the Giants and the Yankees. In college football, the goal posts are moved ten yards back from the goal line.

In 1928 starts the *Big Six Conference* (later to become the *Big Eight*).

In 1929 Green Bay Packers, led by coach Curly Lambeau, win the national title; they play in a small city but are not a real surprise: between 1921 and 1928 they have always ended between the third and the sixth rank.

We will hear more of them.

THE NAMES

DOMINIC «DOM» ALBANESE

Role: *FB/E*
College: *None*
Pro Experience:*1925 Columbus Tigers (NFL)*
Games: 3; Passing: 1–1, Yds 65

Notes:
For him some games in the Columbus team which will play only a few road games in 1925, with terrible results (0–9–0).

RAYMOND «RAY» BARBUTI

HB
Syracuse
None
1927 400 mt. Track&Field USA Champion
1928 Amsterdam 400 mt. and 4x400 Olympic Champion
NIASHF Hall of Fame

On the fields of Lawrence High a young son of «paisanos» runs, jumps, beats hard: he is a horse of breed. In a single football game he reaches eight times the end-zone.

In 1925 he lands to Syracuse University, where he studies, plays football and treads the athletics tracks; good performances, quality playing and interesting timings, a hot temperament.

In 1927 is the captain of a college football team and, at the same time, a national champion of track & field.

And this is how a shining Barbuti grabs the ticket to 1928 Olympics at the U.S. trials.

3014 athletes, representing 46 nations, will arrive to Amsterdam to dispute, between the 17th of May and the 12th of August, the 9th edition of the Games.

In Holland Ray Barbuti is one of the «responsibles» for the final victory of the Americana «dream team», ending up with a booty of 56 medails; in the Olympics dominated by the presence of Paavo Nurmi and from the stir caused by the admission of women to athletics contests, the Syracuse runner will lift the mood of the Americans—who had surprisingly been smashed by canadian Percy Williams both in the 100 and in the 200 metres race—by winning the 400 metres race and the 4x400 medails. In this last discipline Ray, together with Baird, Taylor and «Bud» Spencer, will also establish a new world record.

At the end of his college career Barbuti will take interest in public adiministration and, during World War II, he will enlist for the Usa intelligence. A silent job, the rest of his life in the half-light.

JIM E. BERTOGLIO

FB-WB
Creighton
1926 Columbus Tigers (NFL)
Games:7; Rushing: 3, Yds 5, TD 1; Points 6

A single mark in the NFL record book, one TD in the only season victory of the Tigers (1–6–0) against di Jim Thorpe's Canton Bulldogs. The game will end with the score of 14–2.

GIOVANNI JOHN A. "JACK" BONADIES   <u>**Born in Italy**</u>

G-T
None
1926 Hartford Blues (NFL)
Games: 4

He is third Italian in the 1926 Blues led by Jack Koegh, formerly an assistant coach at Pennsylvania University.

Bonadies will play a bit more the others in a difficult season.

Giovanni was born in Corleto Perticara, Basilicata (a southern region of Italy), in 1892 and moved to America when he was 5 years old together with his mother Maria and the brothers Giuseppe and Angela Maria, joining father Vincenzo in New Rochelle.

FRANCIS «FRANK» BRIANTE

RB/HB
NY Univ.
1929 Staten Island Stapletons (NFL)
1930 Newark Tornadoes (NFL)
Games: 13; Rushing: 72, Yds 185, TD 2; Receiving: 4, Yds 51; Points 12
NYU Athletics Hall of Fame

In 1927 he is a brilliant fullback for the Violets of NY University. National value.

Inducted to the *New York University Athletics Hall of Fame*.

GUIDO G. CAGLIERI

G
Stanford
None

One of the best athletes in 1929 and 1930 winning team (records: 9–2–0 and 9–1–1), led by famous coach Glenn «Pop» Warner.

CARL «SQUASH» CARDARELLI

C
Central High
1923 Akron Pros (NFL)
1924 Cleveland Bulldogs (NFL)
Games:3

«Squash» was named All-Ohio Center in 1913, when Central High made claims to the State prep football championship and finishing with an 8–0 record.

In 1916 he gets his first semipro contract with the Akron Burkhardts; in the first 2 games he scores 2 FGs.

In 1917 he moves to the new franchise of the Akron Grossvater Pros; during the third game of the season against the Columbus Panhandles, he ends at the Peoples Hospital with a dislocated shoulder because of a game collision. Nothing broken, though. From 1918 to 1924 he will play on with different Akron teams, meeting important players like Fats Henry, Ralph Waldsmith, Fred Sefton, Al and Frank Nasser. In 1925 he lands to the NFL. A few games, then he falls in the dusk of small teams named Marlowes, Maples etc …

The little big history of American football remembers a special afternoon, during a game against the Canton Pros, when Cardarelli blocks two of Jim Thorpe's punts and tips a third.

ANTHONY E. «TONY» CATALANO

G
none
1920 Hammond Pros (APFA)
Games: 1

Only one game (out of the only 3 disputed by his team) in the first tournament of the first real American pro league.

FRANK J. «CIVY» CIVILETTO

WB
Springfield

1923 Cleveland Indians (NFL)
Games: 4

He plays 4 games out of 7 in the team of Cap Edwards, which will end the season with an uncommon number of ties (record: 3–1–3).

CHRISTOPHER «CHRIS» CORTEMEGLIA

WB
Southern Methodist
1927 Frankford Yellow Jackets (NFL)
Games: 2; Rushing: 2, Yds 10

A couple of appearances in a long series of games (team record: 6–9–1). At 210 pounds he is, together with Sully Montgomery (215), the heaviest of the Yellow Jackets.

ERNEST L. «ERNIE» CUNEO

G
Columbia
1929 Orange Tornadoes (NFL)
1930 Brooklyn Dodgers (NFL)
Games: 18

A guard in a large number of games for the second New York team, which in 1930 hits a winning season (7–4–1).

NENO J. «JERRY» DA PRATO

FB
Michigan State
1921 Detroit Heralds (APFA)
Games: 6; Rushing: 22, Yds 30;
1915 All-American
1915 National Top Scorer (points 124)
U.P. Sports Hall of Fame
MSU Athletics Hall of Fame

The title of All-American is a very peculiar feature of American sports, dating back to the early XX Century, much appreciated by the athletes and the young supporters. Its main purpose is to identify positive winning figures, «little heroes» of a year, symbols of strength and devotion to show the entire country.

MSU, Michigan State University, is a college with a prestigious sports history; the football team, the Spartans, has appeared at the end of XIX Century, and in 1811, with the arrival of coach John Macklin, it begins a period of important reachings and innovations: the «perfect season», the very first, dates 1913: all games won, no even result.

Then the first black athlete to be included in a football team (many colleges will begin accepting some more, very little at a time, after WW II).

Then the first player in the history of the school to be nominated All-American, in 1915.

His name? Neno «Jerry» DaPrato, the America-born son of a miner and a housewife come from Italy.

The reason of his nomination? Having been the best realiser of the nation (15 touchdowns, 2 field goals and 28 extrapoints); during one single game he will score 32 points, enthralling the audience and ringing a bell for the press.

Glory is short-lifed, though, and in 1952 a diligent compiler of the college record-book will even «forget» his title and name; an oversight to be corrected only in the Eighties.

DaPrato will also have a short pro career: he will be hired in 1921 by the Detroit Tigers, a team with a really short sports life, in the APFA league.

The American Professional Football Association has organised its forst football tournament in 1920; chairman of the association is legendary «Big Jim» Thorpe, the Indian-origins athlete who had been squalified at the Olympic Games.

In 1922 the board of the teams owners decides to change name to the association: NFL, the National Football League, is born.

Neno DaPrato will move to Parkerburg, PE, the town founded by the ancestors of his wife Elisabeth: there he will work as an administrator of the local Fire Brigade Department.

ROMEO A. «BUCK» DEBUCCI

B
Rhode Island
None
URI Athletics Hall of Fame

In 1927 he is a protagonist both on the football field and in the running tracks. Later he will become the president of the URI Alumni Association and an important support to the Rams for more than 25 years, organizing the athletic successes of the Rhode Island team.

ED DEPRATO

HB
Rice
None
Rice Athletic Hall of Fame

1922 leading football player and track champion.

FRED W. DESTEFANO

FB-WB-BB
Northwestern
1924 Chicago Cardinals (NFL)
1925 Chicago Cardinals (NFL)
Games:4; Rushing: 4, 11 Yds, Avg 2.8, TD 1
1925 NFL Championship

Fred is the first Italian-American to win an NFL title!

In 1925 there's a little of him in the Cards winning the tournament with a record of 11–2–1. The team is led by coach Norm Barry and brightened by the great Paddy Driscoll.

The 1925 title caused a polemic aftermath inside the league and on the press; the Pottsville Maroons had won against the Cards on the 6th of December, surpassing them in the final ranking, but then a game not authorized between the Maroons and the Notre Dame college team cost Pottsville a ban, and the title went to the Cardinals.

JOHN J. DELUCA

G
Delaware
None
Univ. Delaware Athletics Hall of Fame

DeLuca plays at high level with the Delaware Blue Hen between 1918 and 1922. Later he will be General Manager of the Wilmington Clippers (American Football League) throughout the 30s and 40s. His major contribution to the sport, though, will be again with Delaware University, where he will be Chairman of the Athletic Department for more than 25 years.

JOSEPH F. DELMONICO

E
Syracuse
None

1924 starter at Syracuse Univ.

ANTHONY DI MEOLO

G
Pittsburgh
None

1928 Pittsburgh Panthers Captain

VALDO DRAGONE

HB
Everett
None
Everett High School All-Time Team

One of the best players in the history of his high-school.

RALPH R. «NICK» FARINA

C
Villanova
1927 Pottsville Maroons (NFL)
Games: 1

Reserve center in the team led in offense by Tony Latone.

JAMES G. «JIM» FRUGONE

RB
Syracuse
1925 New York Giants (NFL)
Games: 3; Punt: 1, Yds 55

The lightest of the Giants (150 pounds among 8 teammates of at least 200), some seldom apparitions on the field and a good punt. Also for him a mark in the big book of NFL.

GUS A. «HOPE» GARDELLA

FB
None
1922 Green Bay Packers (NFL)
Games: 7; Rushing: 6, Yds

7 games out of 10 for «Hope» in the team of legendary Curly Lambeau.

MIKE GAZZELLA

HB-HC
Lafayette
None
Maroon Club Hall of Fame

Standout football and baseball player at Lafayette (1921–23). College National Champion in 1921 (Lafayette record: 9–0–0). Captain in 1923, he served with legendary coach Jock Sutherland.

PASQUALE «PATSY» GERARDI

E
None
1921 Washington Senators (APFA)
Games: 1

Patsy plays one of the 4 games disputed by the team (record: 2–2–0) in one of the first attempts at bringing pro football in the big Eastern cities.

MICHAEL GETTO

T
Pittsburgh
None
1927 Consensus All-American

He plays with the Pitts Panthers, the team which in those years imposed their supremacy in Eastern Football.

HENRY C. «HANK» GILLO

FB/WB/RB/HC
Colgate
1920 Hammond Pros (APFA) player, head-coach
1921 Hammond Pros (APFA)
1922 Racine Legion (NFL)
1923 Racine Legion (NFL)
1924 Racine Legion (NFL)
1925 Milwaukee Badgers (NFL)
1926 Racine Tornadoes (NFL)
Games: 44; Rushing: 324, Yds 1.314; TD 10; Punting: 11, Yds 144; Kicking: PAT 18; FGs 22;
Total Points 144.
1922 NFL Scoring Leader.

He was the first athlete in the history of Colgate University to sign a pro contract. In 1922 he was the best scorer of NFL with 52 points. His team, the Racine Legion, ends the year with a record of 6–4–1.

For Gillo 7 years on the gridiron with the pros in the early years of the Great League.

PASQUALE «PATSY» «JULE» GIUGLIANO

BB
None
1923 Louisville Breks (NFL)
Games:1

The lightest of his team (hardly 135 pounds); a fugace apparition.

DAVID GUARNACCIA

HB
Harvard
None
Harvard Varsity Club Hall of Fame

1927–1929 leading player

GEORGE A. «CHICK» GUARNIERI

E
Canisius
1924 Buffalo Bisons (NFL)
1925 Canton Bulldogs (NFL)
Games: 12; Rec. 8, Yds 127; TD 2; Punt;10, Yds 427

A skilled receiver who completes 2 TDs in his first year, during the up-and-down season of the Bisons (6–5–0).

In 1925 he moves to the Canton Bulldogs together with teammate Pete Calac.

ANTHONY «TONY» LATONE

FB-WB-TB
None
1925–28   Pottsville Maroons (NFL);
1929   Boston Bulldogs (NFL)
1930   Providence Steamroller (NFL)
Games: 65;Rushing: 744, Yds 2.648, Avg 4,2, TDs 26; Rec.: 19, Yds 262; Int. 22;
Points 162

Before football, no sporting clubs, no Irish friends, no college. Twelve hours a day working down the mine.

The Italian father has crossed the ocean, has found a job as a miner, has married a girl from Lithuania, has fixed up a wooden hut, has had a male son, moved from Illinois to the Anthracite Region of Pennsylvania, has fixed up a second wooden hut.

He has digged and digged and digged, and then he is dead.

Tony, orphan of his father at the age of eleven, starts working in the only way the hole he lives in allows: a young trasnsporting miner.

Six days a week, 72 neat hours, pushing carts, then, on sundays, the oval ball. The rest is celebrated with some mud, a sprinkle of sweat and a spill of blood.

The Spaghetti-Slavebaltic-American is trained to move whatever; he excels in the most physical aspects of the only football he knows: great tackler, great hole maker for his teammated in the battle of the lines, great ball bearer.

Pro football, which only from a few years has moved his steps in America, will represent for Tony Latone a chance to catch the tail of life, turn it upside down and live outdoor, in the sun, gaining some more comfort.

He will spend four years in Pottsville, playing in the NFL with the Maroons, aside of many players coming from the Ivy League colleges, while he has barely seen the fifth grade. His team, built up in Pennsylvania, will rank for two years among the very best of the league.

In 1929 the ownership of the team leaves Pottsville and moves to Boston, bringing along the best players to found a new team: the Bulldogs. Tony will play one year in Boston and thene will sign up for the Providence Steam Roller, in search for the last good hire. In the six years of his pro career he has made more than 700 carryings, summing up 27 touchdowns.

The annuals register his decisive performance in the December of 1925, against the famous college team of Notre Dame (then one of the best colleges in America).

After storing away shoes and bumper, Latone will move to Michigan, where he will start a business wirh a former comrade of camp battles; for many years he will use one of the boxes of the Detroit stadium, enjoying the great games of modern football.

Red Grange, one of the first and shiniest pro football stars has once declared about Tony Latone: *«He was a big devil come out from the hell of mines, the most powerful football player I have ever seen».*

JOHN «MAGGIE» MAGNABOSCHI

FB-HC
Indiana
None
1928 All-BigTen Conference
1929 All-American

Gratuated in 1929 at Indiana, High School star athlete in baseball as catcher, in football as fullback. In his college years he will be an All Conference; later he will become one of the best pros of the nation.

He also coached at Clinton High for 4 years (record 35–3–2) winning 2 State Championship; as the head coach of the Ball State University Cardinals he will lead the football team from 1936 to 1957 (68–46–14); in 1945 he will know an undefeated season (8–0–0).

RAYMOND C. «RAY» MARELLI

G
Notre Dame
1928 Chicago Cardinals (NFL)
Games: 2

From Notre Dame to a definitely loser team (1–5–0). As a teammate the 41 years old Jim Thorpe who will dispute only few minutes in the whole season: the *Thanksgiving Day* game lost 0–34 against the Bears.

This was Thorpe's NFL final apparence and *Associated Press* reported: «*In his forties and muscle-bound, Thorpe was a mere shadow of his former self*».

PASQUALE F. «FRANK» MATTEO

T/G
Syracuse
1922   Rochester Jeffersons (NFL)
1923   Rochester Jeffersons (NFL)
1924   Rochester Jeffersons (NFL)
1925   Rochester Jeffersons (NFL)
Games: 17

4 years of beatings and defeats with the everlosing team of Rochester.

NICHOLAS J. «NICK» NARDACCI

RB/WB
W. Virginia
1925 Cleveland Bulldogs (NFL)
Games: 2
1922 All-American

In 1922 he is a leading player of West Virginia and one of the best in the whole country. A very small mark in the NFL yearbooks.

JAMES V. «JIM» PALERMO

G/C
Missouri
1925 Kansas City Cowboys (NFL)
1926 Kansas City Cowboys (NFL)
Games:3
1925 Missouri Valley Conference Champion

Jim Palermo plays with the Missouri Tigers from 1922 to 1925; the latter will be a great season, bringing to a conference title. Afterwards, some battle on the lines of NFL.

PASCAL P. PALERMO

HB
Tulane
None

1924–25–26 Tulane leading player.

WILLIAM «BILL» PASSUELLO

G/T
None
1923 Columbus Tigers (NFL)
Games: 3

A winning season with the Tigers (5–4–1). Bill, with his 230 pounds, is the biggest player of the team.

LOUIS C. «PESS» PESSOLANO

T/G
Villanova
1929 Staten Island Stapletons (NFL)
Games: 3

At the age of 22 debuts in the NFL: an up-and-down season, like that of his team (3–4–3).

AL PIEROTTI

C-G-T
Washington & Lee
1919 Cleveland Tigers (Ohio Pro Team)
1920 Akron Pros (APFA), Cleveland Tigers (APFA); Boston Braves (National League)
1921 New York B. Giants (APFA); Boston Braves (National League)
1923 Milwaukee Badgers (NFL); Racine Legion (NFL)
1924 Milwaukee Badgers (NFL)
1926 Boston Bulldogs (NFL)
1927 Providence Steamrollers (NFL)
1929 Boston Bulldogs (NFL)

Games: 47; Rushing: 2, Yds 10; Passing:3–6, Yds 46; Punt: 2, Yds 107, PAT 2; Points: 2

Al (Albert Felix) comes from Boston, Massachusetts; he is a true pioneer, one of the first athletes to play as a pro of baseball and football at the same time.

He has already been a protagonist during college: at W&L he was a star in baseball, football, track and basket. He was captain of the teams of baseball and football; he was elected All-American in 1916; the following year he led the basket team to a winning streak of 13 victories and no defeat.

Once become a pro, he plays 2 years in the baseball leagues and 9 more years with football teams.

On the 100 yards gridiron he is a good center, an experienced guard, a fighting tackle; in 1920 he plays a game with the Akron Pros, champions of the league, and in the same year he is a player (6 games) and a coach with Stan Cofall in the Tigers.

JOSEPH W. PINTO

BB
Rhode Island
None
URI Athletics Hall of Fame

1925 leading player at Rhode Island State College, in football, baseball, and basketball.

Later he will become a coach, a referee and a teacher, devoting to the education of mentally retarded young adults in New York.

FELIX PLASTINO

B
Idaho
None
ISU Athletic Hall of Fame

1923–24 leading player at Idaho University.

RUDY F. «ROSEY» ROSATTI

T
Michigan
1925 Cleveland Indians (NFL)
1924; 1926–27 Green Bay PAckers (NFL)
1928 York Giants (NFL)
Games: 45

In 1922 he plays as a right tackle and becomes champion of the conference with Fielding Yost's Michigan University team.

He plays 5 years in the NFL; in 1927 he gets on the field 7 times out of 10 games played by the Packers, rank number 2 in the tournament.

SAM «SMOKE» SALEMI

WR
Columbia
1928 New York Yankees (NFL)
Games:5; Rec:: 3, Yds 66; TD:1

His nickname dates back to high school; his teammates admire his defensive qualities and is ability to close all passages like a cloud of smoke.

Once in the Columbia team he plays with legendary Lou Gehrig, who will soon leave the oval ball to start a shiny career over baseball diamonds .

Sam will decide to complete his studies at Casinius College and in 1928 will sign a contract with the NFL team of the Yankees (the one founded by C.C. «*Cash and Carry*» Pyle). His pay will be 125 dollars a game.

He will complete his first and only pro season with a personal record of 5 games, 3 receivings (66 yards) and 1 TD; a good result, considering the seldomness of TD passes of his time.

In 1945 Salemi decides to change his surname into Dana, worried by the frequent misspellings of his.

NFL loses track of Sam in the July of 1969.

His son Bob, a retired schoolteacher, writes to the Pro Football Hall of Fame informing them that the League has mistaken his father with another Salemi, and proving that his father is actually the oldest «pioneer pro» still alive.

In 2004 Sam tore the 100 years ticket!

JOSEPH «SCANLON» SANTONE   **Born in Italy**

G
None
1925 Hartford Blues (NFL)
Games:2

Born in Campobasso (Italy) on the 1st of October 1893, he plays 2 games with the Blues. The team is an open canteer (players coming and going all the time) and ends the season with a 3–7–0 record. Hartford will be Santone's definitive stop: he will live there his whole American life.

ARMANDO SEGHETTI

C
St. Mary's
None

1925 Captain St. Mary's College, (this year 4° in national ranking with 8–0–1 record)

ROCCO «ROCKY» SEGRETTA   **Born in Italy**

E
None
1926 Hatrford Blues (NFL)
Games : 1

Born in Italy in 1899. Also known as «Rocky Segrito», he will register a quick appearance in the NFL, just lie his teammate Santone.

JOSEPH «BUTCH» SPAGNA

G/T
Lehigh
1920 Buffalo All-Americans—Cleveland Tigers (APFA)

1921 Buffalo All-Americans (APFA)—Philadelphia Quackers (Ind.)
1924 Frankford Yellow Jackets (NFL)
1925 Frankford Yellow Jackets (NFL)
1926 Philadelphia Quackers (AFL)
Games: 32(in NFL)
1926 AFL Champion

In 1919 he is involved in the first semi-pro games. He is a natural born warrior, trained to play at least two tough games a week, on saturdays and sundays; in 1921 he is one of the protagonists of the debate about players disputing games on too many fronts, and the League asks him to choose only one team. Butch will decide, together with Lou Little (aka Luigi Piccolo), to complete the season with an independent team, the Philadelphia Quackers.

Throughout 1924 and 1925 Spagna is one of the best known elements of the Yellow Jackets, champions in two tournaments with winning records of 11–2–1 and 13–7–0, ranking third and then sixth at the end of the season.

In the June of 1926 the formation of the AFL (*American Football League*) was announced. The new league will try to break the dominance of NFL.

Leo Conway will bring back the Quackers, out of the games from before the 1922 season; apart from Butch Spagna, more reliable veterans will come back, such as Lou Little, Heine Miller, Johnny Scott, Lud Wray. The season witnesses a good game, a bucketful of determination and the arrival of the AFL title, the NY Yankees behind the Philadelphia team.

JOHNNY P. «BIFF» TOMAINI

E/T
Georgetown
1929 Orange Tornadoes (NFL)
1930 Newark Tornadoes (NFL)
1931 Brooklyn Dodgers (NFL)
Games: 35; Rec. 7, Yds 145, TD 1

In 1927 he is one of the most productive players of the Georgetown University; the team, led by Lou Little, ranks 7th nationwide, with a record of 8–1–0. Once become a pro, Biff will play for three years in NFL, showing a good continuity.

SILVIO TURSI

E
Molhenberg
1927 Staten Island Stapletons (Ind. Pro Team)

Few games in minor leagues scene.

R. J.»RUBE» URSELLA

FB-WB
None
1920 Rock Island Independents (APFA) player-captain-coach
1921Minneapolis Marines (APFA), player-coach
1924 Rock Island Independents (NFL)
1925 Rock Island Independents (NFL) player-coach
1926 Akron Indians—Hammond Pros (NFL)
1929 Minneapolis Redjackets (NFL)
Games: 46; Rushing: 105, Yds 284; Rec. 21, Yds 91; Punting: Punts 69, Yds 2,404, Avg 34,8; PAT 15, FG 6; TD 5.
Coach: 1920:4–2–1;1921: 1–3–0; 1925:5–3–3;

After having been a local hero in Minnesota, played with the Cleveland Indians (American Pro League) and received a nomination as the Ohio League best «sniper» (he scored 99 points during the season, the top total for a major team in 1919), Ursella plays and coaches both in the APFA and in NFL, revealing himself as a good runner, a punctual receiver, an extremely precise kicker, a polyvalent athlete, very much loved by the supporters of the home games played in Douglas Park, Rock Island. As a coach he engages Bobby «Rube» Marshall, the first black player to appear in a league game. In 1926 the Akron team gains the only victory of the season thanks to a 40 yards TD carry of the «Barrell-chester» (one of his many nick-names).

(Towards the end of the Sixties hall of famer Jimmy Conzelman will remember: «*Rock Island was a great football town in those days. The fans really supported us. We drew big crowds for the era … *»)

GEORGE A. VERGARA

E
Notre Dame
1925 Green Bay Packers (NFL)
Games: 12; Rec.2, Yds 32

Started from the Fordham University of Bronx (New York), he lands to Notre Dame's ambitious football program in 1922. In his first season Vergara plays 9 games as a right end; in 1923 he plays as a guard and Notre Dame ends the season with a 9–1 record; in 1924 he wins all the 10 games of the season with the Irish, graduates National Champion and, by the end of the year, becomes freshman football coach and gets his diploma.

In 1925 he plays as a pro with the Packers and becomes interested in politics. He will one day be the mayor New Rochelle, New York.

RAFFAELLO RALPH D. VINCE   **Born in Italy**

E-G-T
Washington & Jefferson
1923 Cleveland Indians (NFL)
1925 Cleveland Bulldogs (NFL)
1926 Cleveland Panthers (AFL)
Games: 15 (NFL), 1 (AFL)

Teammate at W&J of Bird Carroll and Paul Hogan, once become a pro Raffaello lands to Cleveland, where he plyas in 3 teams and 2 leagues. In his first NFL season he plays 7 games and is one of the most displayed among the Indians; he will repeat himself with the Bulldogs: 8 games in 1925. He will end his career a bit "crumpled" in the AFL.

Ralph Vince (a very American name and surname) was born in Vinci, in Italy, in the March of 1900. A new century and a new life.

ANDY ZAZZALI

E
Georgetown
None

He plays with the great 1921 team led by Albert Exendine to a final record of 8–1–0.

THE THIRTIES

BACKDROP

In 1930 the Green Bay Packers win their second national title. George Halas for this year confines himself to the business administration of the Chicago Bears and after 11 consecutive years leaves to someone else the coach bench; in the meanwhile he has engaged a Minnesota University *All-American* named Bronko Nagurski. **Mike Stramiello** is well-seen by the press.

In 1931 the Packers win their third NFL in a row; the New York Giants put under contract Mel Hein, a talented center who will not miss a single game in 13 years of career!

An audience of 40,000 witness the game Giants—Packers disputed at the Polo Grounds. The Big Depression shows its teeth and many teams go bankrupt: Minneapolis, Newark, Franckford, Providence. The best of the season: Dutch Clark, Ernie Nevers, Red Grange, Red Badgro.

In 1932 the Bears win the championship; it has been a season marked by bad weather and snowstorms. Carl Hubbard, Walt Kiesling, Dutch Clark and Bronko Nagurski are the best athletes of the year. **«Jack» Cannella** shows some great game in Fordham; he will play as a pro from the year after and later will become a judge of the Federal Court.

In 1933 are organized the *East* and the *West Division*; a new kind of football is introduced, easier to pass with one hand. In the same year the *Southeastern Conference* comes into being. Rookie **George «Moose» Musso** lands to the NFL: he will play 13 seasons without a break and will make it to the *Pro Football Hall of Fame*. In Canada begins the «Era of Imports», when Canadian teams engage pro and o semipro American athletes.

In 1934 at the Soldier Field of Chicago takes place the first *College All-Stars Game*; Noble Kizer, coach of Purdue, leads the college selection against the 1931 NFL champions Chicago Bears, before more than 79,000 people. **«Scaggie» Ciccone** is a little star, he figures in the cards; **«Nick» Niccolai** plays the first of his 9 seasons as a pro: for many years in a row he will be the NFL best kicker.

In 1935 are designated the first *Heisman Trophy* and the first *Coach of the Year Award*. In the same year Miami hosts the first edition of the *Orange Bowl* and New Orleans the first *Sugar Bowl*.

In 1936 debut both the *Pro Draft* and the *NFL All Stars*; first choice Berwanger will refuse to play football as a profession, considering the pays of his time not gameing his ambition. In 1936–1937 a new league tries to counter the dominion of NFL: the *American Football League*. It will not last long.

In 1937 it is the turn of the first *Cotton Bowl*, played in Dallas. The third Heisman Trophy is won by Clint Frank of Yale, who during the banquet stands up to talk and opens his speech saying that *football is only a nice game; from now on I will have other things to do*. In the years to come he will find a lucky spot in advertisement, and his company will become one of the 20 best ad companies of the United States. George Musso is the first Italian-American to be included in the *NFL All-Pros* voted by all the coaches of the league; **Al Nichelini** is one of the best players of the AFL season; **Gene Ronzani** is on the field the 12th of December to dispute the *NFL Championship Game* (Washington Redskins—Chicago Bears 28–21).

In 1938 the rooster is fixed to 30 units; Sammy Baugh and Ace Parker are the new stars in pro football; the Pittsburgh Pirates engage young Whizzer White for 15,800 dollars: it is the highest pay of the league. **Johnny Dell'Isola** is among the winners of the *NFL Championship Game* (NY Giants—Green Bay Packers 23–17); the following year he too will be selected for the *NFL All-Pros*, the second «Italian» to receive this honour after the advent of pro football.

In 1939 Bert Bell, the former commissioner and owner of the Philadelphia Eagles, engages QB Davey O'Brien of the Texas Christian University and has him insured against any injury by the Lloyds Company of London!

In the same year in Montgomery, Alabama, a selection of players form the Northern colleges meets a selection of the Southern colleges in the first edition of the *Blue-Grey Game.*

QB Neil Kinnick of Iowa, winner of the Heisman Trophy, renounces to a 10,000 dollars engagement with the Brooklyn Dodgers, choosing instead to become a lawyer and maybe a politician; in the June of 1943 he will diappear at sea during a wartime training flight. On the 10th of December in Milwaukee, **«Flash» Falaschi** talkes part to the *NFL Championship Game* (Green Bay Packers—NY Giants 57–0). **Vic Bottari** scores all the points of the *Rose Bowl.* **Bruno «Bree» Cuppoletti** is on the field during the first experiment of TV football broadcasting.

The athletes of Italian origins grow in number year after year, but often are only «cannon fodder» in the battles of the lines, a few and extremely tough games for a bunch a dollars more; sometimes they are massive, ready fot the handfight, but also shrewd and funny. This generation has the luck of knowing good schooling and learning correct American; thanks also to the many religious institutions offering a chance to study also to boys whose families, always poor and often completely illiterate, have lived the tragedy and the hopes of immigration. Some of these boys have been immigrants themselves, outplaced yet wide-eyed and perceptive, ready to catch every single chance to build a better future away from deprivations and misery.

Some others come from families already established in commerce and can afford prestigious universities of the East or in California; in college football the roles are not so rigid and some young Italian-Americans get to play with more continuty in quality teams, conquering national recognition.

Sometimes they will manage to lead also in the pro leagues.

As to Canadian football, in the 1934 *Grey Cup* the score of the team led by **Art Massucci** is enriched by five singles. They are the last drop kicks to be seen in a Grey Cup game. (To the uninitiated, a drop kick was the art of a player dropping the ball and kicking it just as it hit the ground. With the advent of Americans coach in Canada, the drop-kick disappeared in favour of the field goals and converts). Massucci and the Imperials win in 1936 their second Grey Cup in 3 years against the Ottawa Rough Riders (26–20), in a very tense moment for Canadian football: split into an Eastern and a Western organization, it suffers from dirty tricks caused by the sudden changes of the rules (often in the very course of the season).

Other paisanos playing in Canada?

Enrico «Henry» Garbarino, a Montreal Winged Wheelers player, is the first *italiano* to win in 1931 the Grey Cup.

Rocky Parsaca gets hold of 2 Grey Cups in 1934 and 1936; **Bill Ceretti** also wins 2 editions; **A.J. De Diana** is among the regulars of the team that wins in 1933 against the Argonauts; **Austin Del Frate scores** 6 points in the 1932 finals. Yet the greatest of them all was **Johnny Ferraro**, landed to Hamilton in 1934 in the double role of player and coach; he will be remembered as one of the best players of his times and in 1966 will be inducted to the *Canadian Football Hall of Fame*.

THE NAMES

FRANK M. ABRUZZINO

LB-FB-C-G
Colgate
1931 Brooklyn Dodgers (NFL)
1933 Cincinnati Reds (NFL)
Games: 23; Int.:1

Guard and center in cohabitation with Red Bultman in the disastrous team of Brooklyn (2–12–0); in 1933 he signs with one of the 3 NFL new expansion teams: a good season as a center.

MIKE ADAMO

G-T
Lafayette
1937 Newark Tornadoes (AA)
1937 AA Southern Division Title
1937 AA Championship Game

Adamo plays a good season, as his team, which ranks first in the division and ends the season with a tie against the White Plains Bears (3–3). For him 6 points in the regular season and in the record bock.

ROBERT «BOB» ALBANESE

QB
Rhode Island State
1939 Providence Steamrollers (AA)

A short apparition in the American, in cohabitation with Red Kidd. Albanese plays with Mario Tonelli.

VINCENT MICHELE «VANNIE IRON MAN» ALBANESE

FB-LB-DB
Syracuse
1937 Brooklyn Dodgers (NFL)
1938 Brooklyn Dodgers (NFL)—Paterson Panters (AA)
Games: 18; Rushing: 48, Yds 150, Avg 3,1(NFL Stats)
All-Time Players Syracuse

In 1935, during a famous game won 7–3 against Notre Dame, «the unbreakable Iron Man « (as he was defined by contemporary press) puts on scene a startling one-man show, completing a TD 2 minutes before the end of the game which saw him carrying the ball 19 times. The durable Albanese continues to excel also in 1936, when he is the captain of the team. He plays as a pro both in NFL and in the American Association. In 1939 he is on field during the AA Championship, lost against the Newark Bears.

A. AGOSTINI

HB
Marquette
None

A quality back in the strong 1932 Marquette University team.

A. AMATO

G
Oregon
None

1935, 1936, 1937 leading player at Oregon ; 1937 team captain.

PETER «PETE» AMICO

HB
J.Carroll
None
J.Carroll University Athletic Hall of Fame

Leadind scorer on football team in 1930; winning player in basketball from 1929–1931

ETTORE ANTONINI

E
Indiana
1937 Cincinnati Bengals (AFL)
1936 All-American
1936 College All-Stars
1945 Coach of the Year

A protagonist behind the lines of the early Thirties Indiana University team (*All-State. All BigTen, 1935 East-West Shrine Game*). In 1936 he is among the players selected for the first edition of the Pro Draft (he will be chosen by *American Football League*). In 1937 he plays in the second pro league composed by 6 teams (Cincinnati Bengals, Los Angeles Bulldogs, Rochester Tigers, New York Yankees, Boston Shamrocks and Pittsburgh Americans).

In the same year he accepts the place of Assistant Football Coach at Central High School, Muncie; he will keep it until 1944, then will become the Head Coach from 1945 to 1961, with an overall record of 82–46–6, 5 North Central Championships and more awards. During his career he has discovered and trained many *All-State* athletes and also two pros: Gen Flowers and Joe Dooley, who later played with Philadelphia Eagles and Los Angeles Rams.

MIKE ARTALE

HB
J.Carroll
None
1934 Small College All-American
1932–1934 All Big Four halfback
1932–1934 All-Ohio
John Carroll Athletic Hall of Fame

Leading halfback at John Carroll for four years. One of the best college players both in his conference and in the state of Ohio. For him also an All-America nomination.

EDWARD C. «ED» ASPATORE

T-G
Marquette
1934 Cincinnati Reds (NFL)
1936 Los Angeles Bulldogs (Ind./AFL)
1939 Louisville Tanks (AFL)
Games: 6(NFL)

A worthy tackle in the 1932 Marquette University team. A giant in the line of giants of Cincinnati. Unfortunately the season is a disaster, ending before time. After that, Aspatore will try for a couple of years the AFL fields.

MIKE BACCARINI

HB
USF
1937 Salinas Packers (Ind./AFL)
Games:4; Rushing: 9, Yds 28, TD 1

First a good college experience with the San Francisco University; then some pro time in South California, playing for independent teams and in the AFL.

ANDY BARBIERI

G
NYU
1938 Union City Rams (AA)
1939 Union City Rams (AA)

Plays with the Rams, of Sam Zuccaro, a satellite team of the Brooklyn Dodgers.

RICHARD «DICK» BASSI

G
Santa Clara
1937 Salinas Packers (Ind.-AFL)
Santa Clara Football Hall of Fame
1935–1944 Sugar Bowl All-Stars

Outstanding player at Santa Clara; he plays the 1936 Sugar Bowl. In the same year he is called to take part in the Chicago College All-Stars; Richard and his teammates beat the Green Bay Packers 6–0. A parade-game, true. Yet all the same …

ED BELLA

HB
NYU
1936 White Plains Bears—Stapleton Buffaloes (AA)

A couple of contracts in one season, his personal scoring at zero points.

JOE BENEDETTI

G
Columbia
1939 Providence Steamroller (AA)

In 1939 plays with the Steamrollers, second in the Northern Division.

JOE BERARDELLI

T
Ohio State
1939 Newark Bears (AA)
1939 AA Southern Division Title
1939 AA Champion

A good college career, a title conquered in his first pro year in the minors with the Bears.

ANGELO BEVEVINO

WB-QB
Carnegie Tech
None

1933 leading player with the Tartans of Carnegie Tech (Pittsburgh, PA) led by coach Howard Harpsters (1928 All American with the same college).

EDWARD B. BIANCHI

G
SMU

None

1938–40 starter at Southern Methodist University

JOHN L. BIANCONE

RB-DB-QB
Oregon State
1936 Brooklyn Dodgers (NFL)
1938 Paterson Panthers (AA)
Games: 5; Rushing: 8, Yds 34; Passing: 3–1 Yds 29

Teammate of Red Badgro and Joe Maniaci in a not so cool season. In 1938 he plays on the East Coast with the minor league and realizes 1 TD.

JIM "BITS" BIRITELLI

FB-HB
Temple
1936 White Plains Bears (AA)
1937 White Plains Bears (AA)
1938 Clifton Wessingtons (AA)
1937 Northern Division Title
1937 AA Championship Game

In 1936 together with Mazziotti tries to conquer some room in the new league. In 1937 he enjoys the success of the team. The following year he moves to Clifton, the new owners of the Bears.

LOU BORELLI

T-G
None
1936 New Rochelle Bulldogs (AA)

In 1936 plays some down with the team trained by Johnny Scalzi. In 1937 he is a victim of the managerial chaos risking to close the team before time.

NICHOLAS C. «NICK» BORELLI

FB-WB-RB
Muhlenberg
1930 Newark Tornadoes (NFL)
Games: 10; Rushing: 12, Yds 27;Receiving: 2, Yds 43; Pass.: 5–8, Yds 38; Punt: 1,
Yds 35

Only one season, then Newark goes bankrupt. The Big Depression does not spare footall too ...

VIC «VALLEJO» BOTTARI

HB
University of California
None.
College Stats:585 yds rush, TDs 12 (1937); 578 yds and 8 Tds rush, 466 yds and 7 TDs pass (1938);
In three years he has scored 22 TDs, gaining 2.283 yards.
In 1939, decides not to become a pro, despite an offer from the Brooklyn Dodgers.
1940–1941, Marin College coach;
1938 All-American, Pacific Coast Conference champion,
1938 Rose Bowl
(realizes all the pointes of the game; Cal-Alabama 13–0);
War decorated;
All Century PAC10 Team;
Rose Bowl Hall of Fame;
COLLEGE HALL OF FAME

It is a famous, deeply American rivalry the one which marked the yearly games between the college football teams of Stanford and California, way back since 1892. It is the so called «Big game», which has brought on the terraces mounds of supporters (some figures: 82,000 in 1938, 81,000 in 1936, 81,500 in 1948, 83,000 in 1950, 83,000 in 1969, 82.700 in 1975 and so on ...), both for the Cardinals (Stanford) and for the Golden Bears (California).

America's Presidents (Kennedy, Nixon), Olympic gold medals in the field and on the tribunes, famous anchor men from the big networks, stars and starlettes of cinema: they all parade in for the Big Game Week.

And again: full pages on the Bay newspapers, from the *San Francisco Chronicle* to the *SF Examiner*, votations to elect the Wonder Team, the best of the best athletes of the year, anticipations, curiosities, trivia.

A special local week.

Throughout the years the Big Game hosted some of the big figures who would later write the history of sports in all America. First of all the father of American football, Mr. Walter Camp, the coach of Stanford University and the drawer of the first systematic rules of football, those which have marked once and for all the distinction from rugby; then the great Ernie Nevers, a protagonist of the Twenties; famous coach Glenn «Pop» Warner (in Stanford through the Thirties); Clark Shaughnessy, another Cardinals coach who revolutioned the offensive game of football introducing in the Forties the T formation; teh Olympic decatholon champion Bob Mathias (in Stanford for the 1951–52 season); quarterback Joe Brodie, All-America in 1955 and then a protagonist in NFL with one of the greatest teams of history, the San Francisco 49ers; quarterback Joe Kapp, leader of the Golden Bears from 1956 to 1958 and later a player of the Minnesota Vikings (with which will also play the Super Bowl IV); Jim Plunkett, the famous Heisman Trophy awarded quarterback, then protagonist as a pro for the Los Angeles Raiders; coach Bill Walsh, first the head of Stanford and then of San Francisco 49ers; but also John Elway, one of the stars of the Big Game in 1981 and the best leader of a pro offense with the Denver Broncos.

Then, last but not least, Vittorio «Vallejo» Vic Bottari. Who was he?

Son of Italian immigrants come to California to till the earth and produce wine, he was born in Vallejo.

The «country of opportunities» gave him the chance to go to school and get up to the University; in 1936 he is a Cal rookie, and already a regular in the football team, leading the Bears to their first victory in a Big Game in 14 years: it happens on the 21st November at the Memorial Stadium, in front of 81,000 people. Bottari realises a touchdown.

In 1938 it happens again, and this time Vic is the man who makes the winning throw, received directly in end-zone by fellow paisà Angelo Reginato.

The same year Cal wins the Pacific Coast Conference title and the Rose Bowl: in this game Bottari runs 34 times, gaining 137 yards and realising 2 TDs; the same year he gets nominated All-American and is in the rush for the Heisman Trophy. He is one of the nation's best players.

Years later he will be included among the College Football Hall of Fame, among the greatest of all times.

He has worked for an insurance company until 1985, when he retired.

CHUCK BRILLO

T-G
Springfield
1936 Stapleton Buffaloes (AA)

A team with no definitive home stadium and a streak of defeats.

ANGELO «ANGIE» BROVELLI

HB-FB
St.Mary's College
1933 Pittsburgh Pirates (NFL)
1934 Pittsburgh Pirates (NFL)
Games: 13; Rushing: 97, Yds 348; TD:3;Rec.: 6, Yds 137, Avg 22,8
1932 All-American Fullback 1st Team

In some memorable occasions in the Thirties the radio succeeds in making America small. In a gas station, inside a grocery store or in an isolated house, in every corner of the Big Country the Voice arrives to announce some political event, a spectacular incident or a sports game.

The news and populare fantasy run through the prairies, faster than the spirits of the natives, the mustangs and the buffalos; Present and Future come and go swiftly.

In 1939 CBS airs a college football game between St. Mary's and Fordham; the radio commentator is Ted Huring, his voice and his reporting style unmistakable; during the game he will always underline with emphasis the performance of a fullback named Angie Brovelli.

St. Mary's college has a peculiar sports history. Founded in San Francisco in 1863 and then moved to Oakland's suburbs in 1889, St. Mary's adopts football in 1892, only to ban it from 1899 to 1907 because of the many accidents on the field.

Between the Twenties and the Thirties, the Gaels (this is the nickname of St. Mary's players) is protagonist of a string of victories: 9 out of 10 games disputed in 1926; 8 out of 9 in 1929; 8 out of 9 in 1930; 8 out of 9 in 1931; 7 out of 9 in 1934 and 6 out of 8, leading to the victory of the Cotton Bowl, in 1938. At national level, the college team always ranks 3rd to 16th. In 1951 the academic system will dismantle the football program, to reprise, with minor results, in 1968. In the three years 1930–32 it's Angelo Brovelli (1932 All-American) the leader of St. Mary's offense.

For some time his name—that of *Angie the Dark Angel of Moraga*, from the name of the campus—will travel also beyond California. In the temple of New York's Polo Grounds he scores thrice, and the radio is there to tell it.

BILL «BUTCH» BRUNO

QB
Notre Dame
1937 Newark Tornadoes (AA)
1937 Southern Division Champ
1937 AA Championship Game

One of the many talents from Notre Dame, contributing to the good season of the Tornadoes.

JOSEPH E. BUONANNO

HB
Brown
None.
1933 All-American
Brown University Athletic Hall of Fame

He plays from 1932 to 1935 in the Brown University. He is a quality back who makes it to leave a mark on his college recordbook.

I.J. «BABE» CACCIA

G
Idaho
None.
ISU Athletic Hall of Fame

1936–1937 a good football player and wrestler.

ROBERT F. CAMPIGLIO

DB-RB-WB
West Liberty State
1932 Staten Island Stapletons (NFL)
1933 Boston Redskins (NFL)
Games : 17; Rushing: 114, Yds 534, TD 2; Passing: 7–21 Yds 109 TD 1; Rec.: 3, Yds 59, TD 1;Punt Ret.: 19, Yds 165

Bob Campiglio is a valuable college player; in 1929 he is *All-Conference*, in 1930 he is the team's best scorer, boasting a sum of 22 TDs.

He tears the pro foorball ticket with Staten Island, a not very competitive team ending the season last of the list.

In 1933 he moves to Boston, where he gets the chance to play with a couple of two champions like Edwards e Battle. The Redskins end the season with a record of 5–5–0, ranking 3rd in the NFL East.

JOHN M. «JACK» CANNELLA

G-C-LB-T
Fordham
1933 New York Giants (NFL)
1934 New York Giants (NFL)
Games: 11
Fordham University Hall of Fame

Judge John Cannella serves in the Federal Court for 31 years. It was President John F. Kennedy to choose him in 1963.

The son of a Manhattan shoemaker, Cannella dreamt of becoming a doctor, but after he completed a pre-med course at Fordham, the reality of Depression forced him to switch to a less costly career.

Fortunately, John had a marketable skill to help pay his law school bills. A Fordham he was one of the linemen forming the formidable, original «Seven Blocks of Granite» (the same line which, in a later version of 1936, will count on the presence of legendary «paisà» Vince Lombardi). At the end of 2 seasons among the NY Giants pros, «Jack» will receive his Law degree. And a new life will begin.

He will be an assistant to the United States Attorney in the Forties fight to narcos and, later, he will be a lawyer with the Internal Revenue Service in New York.

The judge has lived for many years in the Queens borough of New York, and is dead in 1996, aged 88.

? CAPASSO

G
Brown
None

1933, 1934 Bruins leading player.

JERRY CAPATELLI

G
Iowa
1937 Rochester Tigers (AFL)

Jerry is a regular of the Tigers in the second, hardest year of the new AFL, already deprived of some of its shiniest stars (moved to NFL).

DOMENICO "DOM" "MAC" CARA   **Born in Italy**

E
North Carolina State
1937 Pittsburgh Pirates (NFL)
1938 Pittsburgh Pirates (NFL)
Games: 18; Rec.6, 54 yds

After a streak of good seasons in high school (Bellaire,OH) and in college, Dom is the 10th choice of the Boston Redskins in the 1937 draft.

He will play with the Pirates, instead, and for a couple of years he will dispute a good numbers of games.

Cara was born in Reggio Calabria (Italy) and arrived ti the States when he was very young,

ANGELO CARIDEO

QB-HB
Missouri
1937 Mt.Vernon Cardinals (AA)

A QB with a sounding name, in a team with 4 more QBs. The results are not extraordinaire and the team ranks last in the Northern Division.

FRANK CARIDEO

QB-K-DB
Notre Dame
None
1929, 1930 All-American
1929, 1930 NCAA National Champion
COLLEGE HALL OF FAME

Carideo leads with success the Notre Dame Fighting Irish in a fabulous biennium.

In 1929 the team of Knute Rockne wins the national title under Frank's direction: a perfect season (9–0–0) helloed by an oceanically enthustiastic audience: 90,000 supporters in the game against Winsconsin; 112,000 against Southern California; 80,000 against Army.

During the season Carideo, among many other deeds, makes 5 decisive intercepts, and punt returns for more than 100 yards.

In 1930 Carideo confirms his fame of brilliant player: best quarterback, dangerous runner, strong passer and skilled signal caller; he also excels as a punter. During the first game of the season against Southern Methodist he returns a 45 yards punt directly in touchdown. Notre Dame wins another national title, the third in their history, with a second *en-plein* (10–0–0). Frank receives the second *All-American* nomination.

Throughout the Forties, Carideo is an assistant-coach for prestigious colleges as Purdue (1931), Missouri (1932–34), Mississippi State (1936–38) and Iowa (1939–42, 1946–49).

In the Fifties he will work as an insurance man, and in the Seventies he will retire in quiet Ocean Springs, near a nice golf course.

Among his stats: Notre Dame's top punt returner with 947 yards on 92 returns. In 1951 he will be the first athlete of Italian origins to be inducted to the *College Hall of Fame*.

PETER CARLESIMO

C-G
Fordham
None
Fordham Hall of Fame
University of Scranton Wall of Fame

Player with the Rams in 1937; Football Athletic Director from 1940

Then a long militancy in Scranton: Director of Athletics (1953–1968); Head Football Coach (1944–1960); Head Basketball Coach (1944–1946, 1951–1955).

JOSEPH P. CARLO

T
American
None
AU Cassell Hall of Fame

1938 leading player in football, track and boxing at American Univesity.

WALTER «WALT» CARTE

B
Idaho
None
ISU Athletic Hall of Fame

1936–38: a good player in the Idaho University team.

ERNEST «ERNIE» CASINI

E
Kansas State
1936 Brooklyn Bay Parkways (AA)

1937 Brooklyn Eagles (AA)
1938 Brooklyn Eagles (AA)
1939 Brooklyn Eagles (AA)
1936 AA New York Division Champion

In 1936 he is on the Erasmus Field for the great season of the Parkways, unde-feated in their home. The following year he is confirmed in the team, that changes nickname. In 1938 plays together a certain Vince Lombardi, a tough guard!

RICHARD P. «DICK» CASSIANO

HB
Pittsburgh
1940 Brooklyn Dodgers (NFL)
Games: 10; Rushing 34, 84 Yds; Passing 9–30, Yds 128, TD 1

A sophomore phenom at Pittsburgh, « Dandy Dick» is one of the protagonists of the «Dream Backfield» (Goldberg, Stebbing, Cassiano, Chickerneo), the battery of runners leading the Pitts Panthers on the top of the national ranking in '37. Cassiano, a natural left halfback, plays in that year 10 games, with 69 rushes and 620 yards gained; in 1938 he registers 141 carries for 741 yards gained: the sec-ond best results nationwide.

Chosen by Green Bay in the 4th round, he is put under contract by the Dodgers. For him only one season as a pro.

ANTHONY CAVALLO

HB
Lafayette
None

In 1937 he is a devastating runner, contributing to the 8–0–0 record of Lafayette

DOM CAVELLI

G
Michigan State
1939 East Chicago Indians (AFL)
1940 East Chicago Indians (Ind.)

After a break in 1938, AFL is back with 8 new teams in Los Angeles, Cincinnati, Columbus, Chicago, St.Louis, Dayton, Kenisha and Louisville. For Cavelli & Co., a good season (4–3–0) and a second one played as the one team independent from all leagues, totalising 6 disputed games across Illinois, Michigan, Ohio, Tennessee and Iowa,

TONY CAVELLO

HB
Lafayette
1939 Providence Steamrollers (AA)

A reserve in a battery of valuable backs such as Tonelli,Gintoff e Daddario. He will be remembere for a wild 62 yards run blocked one yard from TD.

CHARLES B. CEPPI

T-K
Princeton
None
1933 All-American
1933 East-West Shrine Game

One of the most qualified players come from the Ivy League in the Thirties; First Team All-America, he is the protagonist of a famous game, the classical Yale— Princeton of 1933 in which, among other deeds, he blocks a punt and then returns it for 45 yards to TD. No significant experience as a pro.

BILL CERIGONE

FB
Bluefield
1938 Danbury Trojans (AA)
1939 Danbury Trojabs (AA)

A young back in Jack Thompson's team, second in the final ranking. Completely different the 1939 season, ending before time because of economic problems.

AL CIAMPA

C
Columbia
1936 New Rochelle Bulldogs (AA)
1937 New Rochelle Bulldogs (AA)
1938 Jersey City Giants (AA)
1937 AA All-League Team (Second Team)
1938 AA Champion

Regular center for the Bulldogs playing in the New Rochelle City Park.

In 1937 he is listed among the league's best player.

In 1938 moves to Jersey City, a satellite team of Tim Mara's Giants. The *Little Giants* will mark the best record of the season (7–1–0), and the American title will be theirs. Only one TD from the adversaries in 8 games.

BEN M. «SCAGGIE» CICCONE

C-LB
Duquesne
1934 Pittsburgh Pirates (NFL)
1935 Pittsburgh Pirates (NFL)
1936 Cleveland Rams (AFL)
1937 Cincinnati Bengals (AFL)
1942 Chicago Cardinals (NFL)
Games: 25 (NFL); 16 (AFL)

«Scaggie» was one of the protagonists of the series of gum cards produced in 1935 by National Chicle.

He chewed bubble-gum but also harsh moments with the Pirates, last in the NFL East in 1934 (2–10–0) and in 1935 (4–8–0). The following year Ciccone moves to AFL and with the Rams completes the first winning season in his career (5–2–2), gaining a deserved final 2nd rank; during the season he plays regularly, also recovering a decisive fumble. In the February of 1937 Cleveland is affiliated to NFL and Ben signs with Cincinnati; that year he will score 6 points. More mature, in 1942 he will return to NFL under the leading star of Jimmy Conzelman.

ERNIE CIPRA

C
Canisius
1936 Boston Shamrocks (AFL)
1937 Boston Shamrocks (AFL)

After the attempts of 1926 and 1934, both ending with an agonistic stop (even if for different reasons), the AFL is back in 1936. Boston is top of the list when the athletes, for economic matters, refuse to dispute the title winning game. In 1937 Boston trips over the failure of Yale much advertised star Larry Kelley, winner of the 1936 Heisman Trophy, who will not play one single down, And Ernie was there all the time.

PHIL CONTI

HB
Dartmouth
1938 Newark Tornadoes (AA)

In a difficult year he will realize 1 TD. With his 150 pounds, Phil is the lightest in the team.

SAM S. CORDOVANO

G
Georgetown
1930 Newark Tornadoes (NFL)
Games: 9
Georgetown Athletic Hall of Fame

Cordovano plays with the Hoyas of Georgetown from 1927 to 1929, then signs for Newark. He doesn't seem to go very far with played football, but in 1946 we find him the owner and general manager of the Buffalo Bisons, a team of the newborn AAFC—*All-America Football Conference.*

Cordovano will remain the head of the Buffalo team (which in 1948 will change name to «Buffalo Bills») until 1949, the year of the AAFC-NFL agreement.

FRANK CORRADINO

G
?
1936 Passaic Red Devils (AA)

A fighter alongside Joe Maniaci.

TOM CORRADINO

G-E
Lafayette
1936 Passaic Red Devils (AA)

The other Corradino playing in Passaic and Clifton.

GENE A. CORROTTO

T
Oklahoma
None
Museum's Sooner Football Advisory Committee

1937 and 1938 team captain. A true leader for the first-over OU football to play in a Bowl Game in 1937.

JOSEPH N. COVIELLO

G-HC
Columbia
None
National High School Hall of Fame
Hudson County Sports Hall of Fame
St.Peter's College Hall of Fame

At the college, Coviello earns a degree in history and plays football. In 1935 he is a leading player at the Columbia, and in 1936 he is the captain of the team.

After the college and a master, in 1938 he starts a career as a coach at Berwick High School (PA). In the period 1943–1946 serves in the Navy. From 1940 to 1960 works as a head-coach and social studies teacher at New York Memorial High School; in the years 1961–1971 he moves to North Bergen High School, always as a head-coach; in the meanwhile he has covered the role of head of State Football Commission. Coviello finishes his coaching career at St.Peter's College in Jersey City, directing the football team from 1974 to 1978.

His is the record of victories in the state of New Jersey, with 254 high school football games won in his career. In his last years he has remained active in the Interscholastics Athletic Associatons.

BRUNO R. «BREE» CUPPOLETTI

G-LB
Oregon
1934 Chicago Cardinals (NFL)
1935 Chicago Cardinals (NFL)
1936 Chicago Cardinals (NFL)
1937 Chicago Cardinals (NFL)
1938 Chicago Cardinals (NFL)
1939 Philadelphia Eagles (NFL)
Games: 66

College football leading player in 1932–1933.

After 5 years of fights in the harsh West division of NFL, Bree finds a contract in the Eastern division of the Eagles.

And together with the Eagles he will be the protagonist of an historical event: the first football game broadcast on TV, on the 22nd of October 1939: the beginning of a new era!

The event takes place at the Ebbets Field of Brooklyn in front of 14,000 supporters (the day before, in the same stadium, for a baseball game of the Yankees were present in 70,000). The «miracle eye› of TV watches the Eagles engage battle with the Brooklyn Dodgers, and Cuppoletti has to look after difficult adversaries such as Ace Parker, Ace Gutowsky and Pug Manders. The game will end 23–14 for the Dodgers.

The players on field will know only too late about the «broadcasting experiment» they have been part of: they thought the game was only transmitted by the usual radio …

Instead in the New York area a few lucky owners of the new magic box had a chance to live, well before time, the great future of TV football.

FRED A. DAGATA

FB
Providence
1931 Providence Steam Roller (NFL)
Games: 1

A meteor in the Providence team, which at the end of the season will end for economical problems; a sad finale for the 1928 NFL champions.

JOHNNY G. DELL' ISOLA

G-LB-C
Fordham
1934 New York Giants (NFL)
1935 New York Giants (NFL)
1936 New York Giants (NFL)
1937 New York Giants (NFL)
1938 New York Giants (NFL)
1939 New York Giants (NFL)
1940 New York Giants (NFL)
Games: 66, Int. 2;
1938 NFL Champion
1939 NFL Divisional Champion
1939 NFL All-Pro
Fordham Hall of Fame

Johnny arrives from the forgery of Fordham; in the New York college he plays three high level years.

As a pro he plays for 7 years in the NFL, winning one national and one divisional title. In 1939 he appears in the list of the best players of the league.

Nat. Chicles also chooses him for their collection of cards, much loved by American boys.

DAVID »DAVE» DE VARONA

T
Stanford
None

In 1937 he is part of the famed «Thunder Team» of Stanford, protagonist of hot *Big Games* against California.

CHRIS DAL SASSO

T
Indiana
None
Indiana Hall of Fame

1935 and 1936 Fightin' Hoosiers leading player, in 1936 he is also the team captain. From 1937 to 1951 he is an Assistant Coach at South Bend, Indiana; from 1952 to 1956 he covers the same role at Indiana University. From 1957 he will be the athletic director of the same college.

D. DELLE TASSE

G
Pittsburgh
None

1937 Pitts outstanding lineman, in the winning team (9–0–1) that will conquer the Lambert Trophy and rank 1st nationwide.

DONALD DE ROSA

HB
Santa Clara
None
Santa Clara Hall of Fame

3 great years (1935–1937); captain of the Santa Clara team in 1936. He will dispute the Sugar Bowl.

LUBY DI MELIO

HC
Pittsburgh
1934 Pittsburgh Pirates (NFL) Head Coach (Record: 2–10–0)

Only one season on the bench, among endless impediments. He is the first Italian-American to lead an NFL team in the Thirties.

ANTHONY «TONY» DI NATALE

K-QB-HB
Boston College
1938 Boston Shamrocks (Ind.-AFL).
1938 Eastern All-Star Team
Boston College Varsity Club Athletic Hall of Fame

DiNatale represents an era for the Boston College Eagles: the era of late Thirties remembered for a legendary, deep and accurate football. He also was a talented QB, captain of the team in 1937.

With the Eastern All-Star team he has faced in a series of exhibition games the best pros of his time.

S. J. DONATO

HB
Penn State
None
Penn State All-Time Player

Captain of the Nittany Lions in 1937.

STEFANO «STEVE» DORA

G
Villanova
1937 White Plains Bears (AA)
1937 Northern Division Champ
1937 AA Championship Game

A good season for this rookie from Villanova.

NELLO D. «FLASH» FALASCHI

FB-LB
Santa Clara
1937 Salinas Packers (Ind.-AFL)
1938 New York Giants (NFL)
1939 New York Giants (NFL)
1940 New York Giants (NFL)
1941 New York Giants (NFL)
Games: 42; Rushing: 2, Yds 10; Rec.: 7, yds 39; KickRet.:2,Yds 32
1936 All-American
1935–1944 Sugar Bowl All-Stars
2 NFL Championship Games
1939, 1941 Pro All-Stars
COLLEGE HALL OF FAME

Driving down Interstate 280 from San Francisco to San José, a small deviation of 8 miles brings to Santa Clara.

There, apart from the Paramount's Great America, the devotees of football go for a pilgrimage to the Santa Clara University, one of the many named alike in California. The University has been founded in 1851 by Jesuits come from Italy, and its first oval ball team has been put together in 1902.

Nowadays the team plays in the Western Football Conference, in NCAA, II Division. Yet from 1936 to 1959 the football played in Santa Clara left an important mark on the history of the college version of the national sport; famous head-coaches and a legion of very good athletes—2 coaches and 2 players in the College Football Hall of Fame, 1 player in the Pro Football Hall of Fame—contributed to the achievements of the Broncos before and after WW II.

Nello «Flash» Falaschi, one of the players to make it to the Hall of Fame, played here from 1934 to 1936; son of two immigrants settled in Los Gatos, at the edges of the first Californian wine-yards, «Flash» studied at the Catholic schools of San José then arrived to the University.

In Santa Clara he proved to be very incisive on the playing field, swift and many-talented, a strong tackler, a great defender behind the lines, an effective ball bearer and also a skillful quarterback.

In 1936 he is discovered by the national press, and at the end of the season he is nominated «All-America Quarterback 1st Team».

Falaschi begins exploiting his leader skills in 1937, when he covers the role of assistant coach for «his» Broncos, who triumph for the second time at the Sugar Bowl.

In the meanwhile comes the call from pro football: the New York team chooses him at the second round of the draft.

In a vortex of scouts, agents, relatives, friends, journalists with double or triple intentions, sporting directors, recruiting directors, first or second round rights sold and bought, TV airings, the yearly rite is performed – waiting for the reprise of the game.

In the world of pro football «Flash» will dispute two Championship finals in four years, gaining another small slice of glory.

TONY FARFELLA

E
North Caroline State
1937 White Plains Bears (AA)
1938 Clifton Wessingtons (AA)
1937 Northern Division Champ
1937 AA Championship Game

1937 AA All-League Team (Second Team)

A great player for the team lead by Mike Banbara. In 1938 moves to Clifton, after the sale of the Bears.

JOE FERRARA

C
Columbia
None
1933 All-American

Together with Cliff Montgomery he is one of the first two All-Americans of Columbia in the Thirties.

ALFREDO «FRED» FIORE

HB
NYU
1938 Paterson Panthers-Clifton Wessingtons (AA)

Debuts with the Panthers and then plays with Wessingtons, a team often mistaken for the old Bears (of which they have bought the contracts).

ANGELO FORTUNATO

QB
Fordham
None

Fordham in 1937 achieved its first undefeated season (7–0–1; National Rank: 3) since 1929, and Fortunato is there.

In 1938 he will still be there when the Rams rank 15 with a recors of 6–1–2, as in 1939 (6–2–0, 17th in the final ranking).

GENE FRANCINI

HB
USF
1937 Salinas Packers (Ind.—AFL)

For one year teammate of Flash Falaschi. The Californian Packers were born in 1936, and immediately received authority from the defeat of the L.A. Bulldogs . In 1937 they are a winning team.

EDMUND «ED DEVIL DOLL» FRANCO

G-T
Fordham
1944 Boston Yanks (NFL)
Games:10
1937 All-American
COLLEGE HALL OF FAME

In 1935 Ed Franco plays with Fordham and is one of the protagonists of the legendary line known as the «Seven Blocks of Granite»: only 2 defeats in 3 agonistic seasons. Apart from Franco, the formidable formation was composed also by Vince Lombardi and Alex Wojciechowicz.

Inl 1935 he is *All-American*, in 1936 captain of the Eastern team in the *East-West Shrine Game*.

In 1944 he debuts in NFL with a new team created in Boston by Ted Collins, to no particular luck.

After his degree he will get back to Fordham as a line coach, and later will work for Vince Lombardi as a scout of the Packers.

FRANK GAMMINO

FB
Brown
None.

In 1932 he is the he is the Bruins' ram; his father turns him on promising 100 $ for every TD.

His family administrates the rich Warren Hotel, and often the restaurant offers sumptuos Italian diners to Frank's teammates. What else is there to say?

EDWARD «EDIE» GATTO

T
LSU
None
1937, 1938 All-SEC Team

Star tackle of the team and of the SEC conference. A couple of memorable years, culminating in the Sugar Bowl game.

JIMMY GATTO

T
Scranton
None.
The University of Scranton Wall of Fame

1934 Scranton team captain. Between 1934 and 1943 head coach at Dunmore High School, then againg from 1946 to 1950. From 1955 he is the Athletic Director of the same school.

JACK M. GIANNONI

E-DE
St. Mary's
1938 Cleveland Rams (NFL)
Games: 3

A quick apparition in the NFL under the temporary guide of Hugo Bezdek, the man who from 1936 was in the same time head trainer of two pro teams of football and baseball. Bezdek will leave the team by the fourth game of the season.

VINCENT «VINCE» GLORIOSO

C
J. Carroll
None
1933, 1934 All-Big Four center
John Carroll Athletic Hall of Fame

Starter in the last team of legendary coach Ralph Vince. Much appreciated by the press; the *Cleveland Press* will include him in the College All-Stars team of 1934.

AL GRILLO

G
Idaho
1937 New York Yankees (AFL)

He is on the field in one of the few prestigious victories of his team: 7th of November 1937, NY Yankees—Cincinnati Bengals 21–13 .

In 1938 he is with the *Little Giants*, leading the seasonal ranking. With his 235 pounds he towers in the middle of the field, and he still is the maximum weight in the team. Same story in 1939, both as weight and, partially, as victories.

MARIO C. «MARNE» INTRIERI

G-T-C-LB
Loyola
1932 Staten Island Stapletons (NFL)
1933 Boston Redskins (NFL)
1934 Boston Redskins (NFL)
Games: 20

At his second year in NFL he signs for the money-losing Boston franchise, whose ownership will pass by the end of the season to George Preston Marshall. The record is 5–5–2. Intrieri, who is the biggest player of the team (250 lbs.) together with Turk Edwards, will play side by side with tailback Cliff Battle, a future hall of famer.

The Redskins play at Fenway Park and often have a modest audience: max 26,000 supporters against the Bears.

JIMMY IPPOLITO

E-K
Temple
1937 Paterson Panthers (AA)
1938 Paterson Panthers (AA)
1939 Paterson Panthers (AA)
1938 AA All-League Team
1939 AA Championship Game

In 1937 Ippolito plays with a team in polemics with the league management. They rank second in the division, and the following year Ippolito is the second best scorer of the American Association with 28 points.

In 1939 he is again one of the best snipers of the league: 6 on 6 in the *extra points*.

BENNY LAPRESTA

FB-LB-DB
St. Louis
1933 Boston Redskins (NFL)
1934 St. Louis Gunners (NFL)
Games: 9; Rushing: 11, Yds 62; Receivin:. 2, Yds 27.

His career in the NFL last with the franchise substituting the Cincinnati Reds during the season. Nothing unforgettable.

MICKEY LEONE

QB
Georgetown
1936 New Rochelle Bulldogs (AA)

Back-up of coach-player Scalzi, also from Georgetown.

VINCENT «VINCE» LIBERTO

E
Manhattan
1936 Mt. Vernon Cardinals (AA)
1937 Mt. Vernon Cardinals (AA)

For Liberto 1TD and a good 1936 season with the Cardinals.

LOUIS L. «LOU» LITTLE (born LUIGI PICCOLO)

T-HC
Vermont—Pennsylvania
1920 Buffalo All-Americans (APFA)
1921 Buffalo All-Americans (APFA)
Games:17
1916 All-American
1933 Rose Bowl (Columbia head-coach)
NIAS Hall of Fame
1943 NY Touchdown Club Award
COLLEGE HALL OF FAME

Little reveals himself as a good tackle during his first year in a Vermont college; the following year (1916) he moves to the Pennsylvania University. World War I stops the games and involves also the United States. Lou will get back to Pennsy in 1919.

2 years and 17 games with the All-Americans in the first pro league, always in the high ranks of the torunament.

In 1924 Little is the new head-coach of Georgetown: 6 seasons and a record of 39–12–4.

In 1930 arrives the call from the famed Columbia University, which hasn't yet developed an interesting tradition in football.

Little will stay at the Columbia fo 27 years (until 1957), becoming famous for some events:

from 1931 to 1934 he will lose only 1 game a season;

in 1933 he will lead his team to a prestigious victory in the Rose Bowl (7–0 against Stanford);

the TD scheme of the Rose Bowl will be hailed by the newspapers; baptized «KF-79», it will be taught for decades to the many new players of Columbia;

he will rememberd in a peculiarly negative way in the writings of Jack Kerouac (the «father» of the *Beat Generation*), who will indicate him as the responsible fort the failure of a high school football promise, a halfback landed to Columbia with a scholarship and great credentials. That promise (and that failure) was Kerouac himself. For many years the writer will regret answering to the call of Lou Little's scouts instead than to the call of Frank Leahy (Boston College).

And it is true that Lou «did not see» Kerouac, yet he discovered and launched two stars like Sid Luckman e Paul Governali; but most importantly, he has determined the first big victory for Columbia. American and world literature owe him a lot … and so do those who suffer from toothache. At Columbia they said that Little, after his graduation from *dental school*, had discovered that the seat and the tools of dentists were built only for right-handed people. For him, born left-handed, the only other option was football …

THOMAS A. LOMBARDI

C
Syracuse
None

1932 team captain. 3 years of prestigious victories for Syracuse (record: 16–7–4).

LEONARD D. MACALUSO

FB
Colgate
None **1930 All-American**
1930 East-West Shrine Game

This outstanding fullback during his senior year led the nation in scoring with 144 points.

During his college years with the Colgate team he brings home a significant record of 23–5–0.

ANTHONY A. «TONY» MANFREDA

WB-RB
Holy Cross
1930 Newark Tornadoes (NFL)
Games: 2; Rush 1, 12 Yds.

A tough season, one victory for his team and none for him.

JOE G. MANIACI

FB-LB-HB-DB
Fordham
1936 Brooklyn Dodgers (NFL)
1937 Brooklyn Dodgers (NFL)
1938 Brooklyn Dodgers—Chicago Bears (NFL)
1939 Chicago Bears (NFL)
1940 Chicago Bears (NFL)
1941 Chicago Bears (NFL)
Games: 60; Rushing: 404, Yds 1,855, TDs 14; Receiving: 16, Yds 184; Kicking: PAT 29–34; FG 5–8; Total Points 134.
Fordham Hall of Fame
1940 NFL Champion

In 1935 he is the captain of the Fordham Rams (6–1–2 e 11° in national rank-ing) and he is the protagonist of some important, winning games in which he gains large slices of field and completes crucial TDs.

After 2 seasons as a regular player of the Dodgers, by the half of 1938 he is engaged by the Chicago Bears: he is to substitute Bronko Nagurski, who has come to a full stop in his career.

With the Bears he will play the 1941 NFL Championship Game against Wash-ington Redskins (a 73–0 victory!) in the Griffith Stadium of Washington D.C.; Joe will complete one TD, running for 45 yards in the first quarter of the game.

The precision of the Bears' T-formation has done wonders, taking no prisoners.

Maniaci will also serve in World War II.

? MANTENUTO

HB
Rhode Island
None.

In 1933, during a game Rhode Island-Maine, he will complete a 100 yards run.

JOE MARINO

G
William&Mary
1937 Brooklyn Bushwicks (AA)
1939 Brooklyn Eagles (AA)

He debuts in 1937 in American Association with the new Brooklyn team (the second after the one set by Harold Lippman).

ANTHONY F. «TONY» MATISI

T
Pittsburgh
1938 Detroit Lions (NFL)
Games : 5
1937 All-American

One of the stars of Pittsburgh in college times.

In the NFL, he is a starter in 5 games of the Lions' winning season (7–4–0, 2nd rank in the West Division, behind the Packers, which was defeated 17–7 by the Lions themselves in the third game of the season: a good celebration for the new Briggs Stadium in front of 55,000 supporters!

HARRY MAZZEI

QB
Villanova
None

Leading player in 1938 (team record: 8–0–1)

TONY MAZZIOTTI

HB
Notre Dame
1936 White Plains Bears (AA)

He is in the record-book for 1 XP point. With him in the Bears roster also other *paisà*: Marra, Martino, Passerella, Paterno, Patella (not Batella) … A little Italy …

JOHN S. MESSINA

HB
Rhode Island
None.
URI Athletics Hall of Fame

Recognized as one of the most extraordinaire athletes in the history of his college, Messina in 1937 dominates football, baseball and basketball. He dies in WWII during the invasion of Sicily (Italy)

JOE MILANESI

T
NYU
1937 Newark Tornadoes—White Plains Bears (AA)
1937 Northern Divisision Champ
1937 AA Championship Game

A top player: plays with the Tornadoes that win the Southern, then moves to the Bears winning the Northern (and disputing the Championship against the Tornadoes).

WILLIAM «BILL» MONTESI

G
None
1937 Danbury Trojans (AA)

Plays in a new team with little audience (no more than 2,000 people per game). Yet the few supporters of the Lee Stadium appreciate this reliable guard.

JOHN MUSCALINO

C-G
Ithaca
1936 Syracuse-Rochester Braves (AFL)

The new edition of AFL looked like a «major league», present in big cities like Boston, Cleveland, New York and Pittsburgh; were engaged some established champions like Red Badgro (who plays with Muscalino himself in the Braves) or college stars like Don Elser, from Notre Dame. Yet the fields tell us a different story: after three defeats Badgro returns to NFL, and after five the Braves abandon Syracuse and move to Rochester. 2 games after (the only victory of the season and yet another defeat) the managers will close up shop.

GEORGE F. «MOOSE» MUSSO

T-G
Millikin
1933 Chicago Bears (NFL)
1934 Chicago Bears (NFL)
1935 Chicago Bears (NFL)
1936 Chicago Bears (NFL)
1937 Chicago Bears (NFL)
1938 Chicago Bears (NFL)
1939 Chicago Bears (NFL)
1940 Chicago Bears (NFL)
1941 Chicago Bears (NFL)
1942 Chicago Bears (NFL)
1943 Chicago Bears (NFL)
1944 Chicago Bears (NFL)
Games: 128
1935 NFL All-Pro
1939 NFL All-Pro (*both in the defensive and in the offense team*)
7 NFL Championship Games (4 titles: 1933, 1940, 1941,1943)
COLLEGE FOOTBALL HALL OF FAME
PRO FOOTBALL HALL OF FAME

Big George Musso, the son of a miner, has been one of the greatest players NFL had in the Thirties and Forties. In 1982 he has been included in the «Glory Ark» of pro football.

The day of the ceremony is a special day, one to remember and to tell the grand-children at all anniversaries, or in one of the many Big George Days at the local schools.

«Moose» has been the first, great polyvalent player to tread the fields, a defensive guard and an offensive tackle of rare efficiency, rocky, fighting, a long course cap-tain.

Once retired, he has worked in the catering and has served for many years as the Madison County Marshall. Every time someone asked him to tell a memorable episode, he has lowered his voice, as a true American, while he underlined that he was the only football player ever to encounter and shake a bit two Presidents to be: in 1929, during the Millikin-Eureka college football game, he played against guard Ronald Reagan, and in 1932 he has crashed against Gerald Ford, Michi-gan's center. He represents the big historical change: the first Italian-American ever to be included in the All-Stars pro selection, in 1937. The NFL's official team of this year was selected by coaches throughhout the league.

DICK NARDI

DB-HB
Ohio Sate
1938 Detroit Lions (NFL)
1939 Pittsburgh Pirates—Brooklyn Dodgers (NFL)
Games: 14, Rushing: Rush 30, Yds 124, Avg 4,1; Passing 2–5, Yds 12; Receiv.:1, Yds 3; Punt 1, Yds19.

His first NFL season is good as the season of his team (7–4–0. Ranking 2nd in the West Division).

The rest is not much.

WILLIAM «BILL» NARDI

OG
J. Carroll
None
1933, 1934 All-Big Four
1935 All-City basketball team

A star in college, where he plays as a starter in a football team for 3 years in an ever-winning team. Nardi, in the meanwhile, is also the leader of the basket team.

«BRONKO» NATTINI

FB
Pacific Normal
1936 Brooklyn Bay Parkways (AA)
AA New York Division Title

In the roster of one of the strongest AA teams.

WARREN «RED» NEGRI

T-G-K
Virginia Tech
1937 Dunbury Trojans (AA)
1938 Dunbury Trojans (AA)
1939 Dunbury Trojans (AA)
1940 Boston Bears (AFL)
1941 New York Americans (AFL)
AFL Stats: XP 12–15; FGs 3; Points 21

A tackle realizing 1 XP point in 1937. In 1938 he is the 6th best scorer of the league (15 points). In 1939 the Dunbury team is disbanded and suspended by the league. Negri will anyway realize 5 points. In 1940 he leaves a mark also in the AFL, with the Bears playing in Fenway Park and ending the season with a good 5–4–1 record.

ALLEN J. «AL» NICHELINI

HB-WB-DB
St.Mary's
1935 Chicago Cardinals (NFL)
1936 Chicago Cardinals (NFL)
1937 Los Angeles Bulldogs (AFL)
Games: 23; Rushing: 149, Yds 423, TDs 4; Receiving: 10, Yds 133, TD 1 (NFL);
TDs 4 (AFL)
1935 Chicago College All-Stars Game
1937 AFL All-League Team
1937 AFL Champion

After the winning years of St.Mary's (1934 captain), Nichelini lands to Chicago, where he completes 5 TDs in little more than 20 games. He will leave a mark also in AFL: 4 TDs, 2 of which after long runs (68 and 62 yards), in only 8 games; one title of league and one election to the end-season All-Stars game.

JOHN NICOLINI

E
Notre Dame
1939 East Chicago Indians (AFL)

The Indians, also known as the Steelmen because of the sponsorship of a steel plant, play an acceptable year with Nicolini. Final record: 4–3–0 .

AL NICCOLAI

G
None
1939 Kenosha Cardinals (AFL)

Niccolai plays a season with the team of Kenosha sponsored by Cooper Underwear.

For the Cardinals a season record of 2–7–0 .

ARMAND «NICK» NICCOLAI

T-G-DE
Duquesne
1934 Pittsburgh Pirates (NFL)
1935 Pittsburgh Pirates (NFL)
1936 Pittsburgh Pirates (NFL)
1937 Pittsburgh Pirates (NFL)
1938 Pittsburgh Pirates (NFL)
1939 Pittsburgh Pirates (NFL)
1940 Pittsburgh Steelers (NFL)
1941 Pittsburgh Steelers (NFL)
1942 Pittsburgh Steelers (NFL)
Games: 97; PAT 71–78; FGs 34/45; Points:173
Duquesne Sports Hall of Fame

A protagonist in Duquesne, led by coach Layden. A long pro career (9 years in the NFL); most consecutive seasons leading league in FGs kicking. Also for him the satisfaction of being portrayed in the Nat. Chicles cards.

REINO O. NORI

RB-DB-QB
Northern Illinois
1937 Brooklyn Dodgers (NFL)
1938 Chicago Bears (NFL)
Games: 7; Passing: 11–23, Yds 168; TD pass 1; Rushing: 27, Yds 82.

A phenom in college; from 1932 to 1936 he is the leader of the basketball, baseball and football teams, and a protagonist in track and field and wrestling.

A quick two-years passage in NFL, blocked from the start by a guy called Ace Parker and then, in Chicago, by Bernie Masterson and some injuries.

JOHN F. «COUNT» ORSI

E
Colgate
None
1929, 1930 Consensus All-American
1931 East-West Shrine Game
All-Time Players Squad
COLLEGE FOOTBALL HALL OF FAME

Orsi is one of the best known athletes of the Colgate University which between 1929 and 1931 marks a record of 25–3–0 beating quality teams like Penn State, Brown and Syracuse. The Italian-American is a quick, smart and reliable receiver; but he can also be an aggressive defender, unforgiven in his tackles. Captain of the 1931 Colgate Team, he also disputes that year's East-West Shrine Game.

From 1932 to 1941, before converting to trading, Orsi works as a coach at Colgate.

JIMMY PACE

E
?
1937 Paterson Panthers (AA)

In 1937 he is the 4th best scorer in the league, and the best receiver together with Reissig.

JOSEPH «DIAMOND» PAGLIA

K
Santa Clara
None.
Santa Clara Hall of Fame

Strong kicker in the first half of the Thirties; one of the most admired athletes in the 1934 Broncos.

TONY V.»TOOTS» PANACCION

T
Penn State
1930 Frankford Yellow Jackets (NFL)
Games: 4

Tony adds to the fields his 220 pounds in a tough season; the team will end with a record of 4–13–1.

MATT PATANELLI

E
Michigan
None
1931,1932 All-State High School
1935, 1936 All-BIG TEN Conference
1936 All-American
Indiana Hall of Fame

A protagonist with Michigan in the college years (1934–36, 1936 Captain). Chosen by the Pirates in 1937, he will not find a place in the NFL.

Later he will be the coach of Western Michigan State (1942–1947 e 1952–1962).

JACK PELLICCI

T
Michigan
1937 Mt. Vernon Cardinals (AA)

A pillar of the team owned by the Mt. Vernon Exhibition Corporation.

BRUNO PELLEGRINI

HB
Santa Clara
None
Santa Clara Hall of Fame

In 1936 he gives his contribution to the great year of the Broncos (8–1–0, ranking 6th nationwide). In the same year he disputes the Sugar Bowl (0–9 against the Texas Christian). He repeats the experience the next year (also ranking 6th with Santa Clara, final record: 9–0–0):

CARLO A. «CARL» PIGNATELLI

HB-FB
Iowa
1931 Cleveland Indians (NFL)
Games: 7; Receiving: 2, Yds 6; Rushing: 4, 7 yds

After college he plays with the semipro team of the Ironton Tanks (state champions in 1927). In 1931 he signs with Cleveland; a distressing season counting 2 prestigious victories against Brooklyn Dodgers and Providence.

JOHN POGGI

T-B
Hobart
1936 Brooklyn Bay Parkways (AA)
1937 Brooklyn Eagles (AA)
1936 AA New York Division Title

Another player in the roster of the Parkways, the team that in 1936 will win their division but will not be able to dispute the Championship against Paterson (winners of the *New Jersey Division)* for organizational reasons. Also for him a second year in the Brooklyn team that in 1937 will change name into Eagles.

NICK PRISCO

HB
Rutgers
1936 Stapleton Buffaloes (AA)

In a not really competitive team Nick is the best player, together with the other HB George Red Cronin.

JULIUS J. RADICE

B
Maryland
None
Maryland University Hall of Fame

In 1930 he is the MVP in 3 sports (football, basketball, baseball).

TOM RANDAZZO

E
St.Francis
1939 Newark Bears (AA)
1940 Newark Bears (AA)
1939 AA Champion

In 1939 realizes 8 receivings for 3 TDs in the satellite team of the Chicago Bears winning the AA Championship Game against Paterson (final score: 27–7).

ANGELO REGINATO

E
California
None
1938 PAC-10 Conference Champion.

Skilled End of the California Golden Bears; one of Bottari's preferred targets; protagonist in the 1938 *Big Game*, when he also completes the winning TD.

VINCENT «VINCE» RENZO

HB
Temple
1938 Paterson Panthers (AA)
1939 Paterson Panthers (AA)
1940 Paterson Panthers (AA)
1938 AA All-League Team
1939 AA Championship Game

A quality 1938: 4 TDs and 3rd best scorer nationwide (the 1st among the backs). In 1939 realizes 2 TDs and gets to the finals, lacking in luck; in 1940 1 more TD for him.

GENE RICCARDI

E
Holy Cross
1936 New Rochelle Bulldogs (AA)
1937 New Rochelle Bulldogs (AA)
1938 Newark Tornadoes (AA)

1 TD for him in his first season in the American Association. After this, nothing else to remember.

JOHN «JACK» RIZZO

FB
Lehigh
None
Penske/Lehigh Athletics Hall of Fame

A punishing fullback at Lehigh; in 1932, 313 yards in a single game, 1,143 yards and 19 TDs in a single season. Also the top sprinter during 4 years, he set school records in both 60 and 100 yards sprints.

TONY RIZZO

T
Pittsburgh
1938 Brooklyn Eagles (AA)

The biggest of his team (240 lbs.) in a swinging season. The Eagles end with a 3–5–1: they won the first 3 games in a row, then the decline.

VALENTINO RIZZO

G
Villanova
None

With the team of Villanova (season record: 8–0–1) he plays the 1937 Bacardi Bowl in Avana, Cuba, against Auburn (final score: 7–7).

CONNIE RIZZOTTI

HB
none
1936 New Rochelle Bulldogs (AA)

In the battery of the runners with Barkus, Hurley and Pitts.

EUGENE «TUFFY» «GENE» RONZANI

QB-HB-DB-LB-FB-HC
Marquette
1933 Chicago Bears (NFL)

1934 Chicago Bears (NFL)
1935 Chicago Bears (NFL)
1936 Chicago Bears (NFL)
1937 Chicago Bears (NFL)
1938 Chicago Bears (NFL)
1939 Newark Bears (AA)
1940 Newark Bears (AA)
1944 Chicago Bears (NFL)
1945 Chicago Bears (NFL)
1947–1949 Chicago Bears (NFL) Assistant Coach
1950–1953 Green Bay Packers (NFL) Head Coach
Games: 78; Rush. 260, yards 1,153, TD 1; Rec. 22, yards 396, TDs 8; Passing: 73–192; yards 1,201; TDpass 15; Int. 21; Defense Int. 4, 19 yards; Total points 57 (player)
Coaching record: 14–31–1
1933 NFL West Division Title
1933 NFL Champion
1934 NFL West Division Title
1934 NFL Championship Game
1937 NFL West Division Title
1937 NFL Championship Game
Marquette Athletic Hall of Fame

A native of Iron Mountain, Michigan, son of a miner from Italy, he asserts himself as a football player at the Marquette University (1931–1933), becoming the team captain in 1932. He is an interesting and versatile athlete: he is also the co-captain of the basketball team and a good javelin thrower in the track & field contests. In 1933 he is chosen by the Bears and immediately hits … Hollywood; he will indeed be cast as one of the protagonists of the movie *Pro Football* directed by Ray McCarey, telling the story of a team of champions (the other «actors being his new teammates Link Lyman, George Musso, Ookie Miller, Zuck Carlson, Bill Hewitt, Bronko Nagurski, Red Grange, Carl Brumbaugh); the move will be on the screens in 1934. The 1933 season of the rookie registers 11 games played out of 13, and a great reaching: the Bears win the conference title and the NFL finals (Bears-NYGiants 23–21) marking the first perfect season in the history of the league.

In 1934 too the Bears dominate the Western (13–0–0); Ronzani, is the best receiver with 3 TDs and the third best runner of the team with 485 yards, behind the 586 of Nagurski and the 1,004 of league leader Bettie Feathers. The Bears go to New York to dispute the title game with some regular player left home for injuries. The field is icy; the Giants, losing by 13–3 at the beginning of the last quarte, surprise everybody by scoring 27 points and become the new champions of the league. The 1935 season sees Ronzani becoming the best runner of the Bears: he gains more yards than Feathers and also shows good things as a quarterback and a receiver; the team from Chicago will end 3rd in its division (6–4–2). In 1936 Ronzani plays 10 games out of 12 and realiszes 2 TDs as a receiver; the Bears rank 2nd and launch some interesting rookies. The following year Gene is on the field 11 times, covering various roles and scoring some good points now and then: he is not the star of the team, but still a reliable interpreter of Halas' football, a good veteran; at the end of the season arrives the divisional title and the NFL finals (lost to the Redskins). 1938 marks the down phase in Ronzani's career: few games played, some forgettable down; the Bears will end their season 3rd (6–5–0) and Gene will play 8 chunks of games without scoring points. It is time to leave fields and start nursing the new players in some farm club. 6 years later, though, the war shakes also the NFL and the Bears call back the mature Ronzani (Aged 35) as the back-up of great Sid Luckman; Gene does his share and register a 26–56 with 448 yards and 9 TD passes. The Bears will rank 2nd in their division. Ronzani will play also in 1945 (10–24, 119 yards).

Between 1947 and 1949 Ronzani will become the assistant-coach of the Bears, sometimes working in the farm clubs controlled by Chicago (Newark, Wichita, Akron). IN 1950 will come the contract as the Green Bay Packers head-coach. A troubled experience, marked by the difficulties of the team in building a competitive roster: there will be 2 years poor in satisfactions (3–9–0 both in 1950 an 1951), followed by an even 1952 (6–6–0) and a nice victory against the Redskins (35–20 the score).

The following year Ronzani will be removed 2 games before the end of the season: he had never been much loved by the fans, mostly because of the dim performances of «his» Bears.

DOMINIC «DOM» ROSSELLI

QB-HC
Geneva
None

NAIA District Championship
NCAA Regional Tournements Champ
NCAA Basketball Playoffs
1956,1957,1958 NAIA National Basketball Tournement Elite Eight
1957 NCAA Division II Coach of the Year
1958 Italian Coach of the Year
1964 Ohio College Coach of the Year

A good quarterback in High School (late Thirties), then a standout football and basketball player for Geneva College After graduating (1939), Rosselli comes to Youngstown College. The first year he is an assistant to coach Beede in the football team; the second year, in the basketball team. Then comes the war and Dom becomes a U.S. Air Force Captain, fighting overseas.

At the end of the war he comes back full-time to Youngstown State University, piling up a series of formidable records.

In 39 years as a basketball coach he will score a stunning record of 589–388; and in the meanwhile he will also be for 27 years a baseball coach and for 20 a football coach. His rate of victories with the Penguins, summing up all three sports, equals to .625!

When he retires in 1982 he will be 10th in NCAA history in lifetime collegiate victories.

RAYMOND «RAY» ROSSO

K
California
None
1937, 1938 PAC-10 Conference Champion.

Regular kicker of the Golden Bears ; present in the *Big Game* record-book (1 PAT in 1939).

GILDO «AL» RUSSO

HB
Georgetown
1936 Brooklyn Bay Park Ways (semipro—Eastern Football League)
1936 EFL Champion

In 1936 Russo completes 6 TDs, contributing to the victory of both the NY Division and the championship.

ANDREW J. «ANDY» SALATA

G—HC
Pittsburgh
1929 Orange Tornadoes (NFL)
1930 Newark Tornadoes (NFL)
1930 Newark Tornadoes (NFL) Head-Coach
Games: 10

Salata signs for a newborn team of New Jersey, founded by the Irange Athletic Club which bought the Duluth Eskimos' inactive franchise and entered the NFL in 1929. Known as the Tornadoes, the team had been successful while playing independently. But could manage only 3–5–4 record. In 1931 the franchise moves to Newark, where it will close dowb after another unlucky season. Record 1–10–1.

During the 1930 season Andy will substitute the two coaches McGall and Fish, covering the double role of player—coach. No significant results (personal coaching record: 0–3–0)

JOSEPH SALATINO

T
Santa Clara
None
Santa Clara Hall of Fame

1935 leading player a Santa Clara.

AMERINO «MOODY» SARNO

T-HC
Fordham
1936 Boston Shamrocks (AFL)
1936 AFL All-Stars

Leading tackle at Fordham. In 1936 he is one of the best players of the Boston franchise taking part in the wobbling AFL; the team is the best of the season, yet its athletes, and Sarno among the, will refuse to play the last game of the season (which would have declared them the official champions of the league) because their wages haven't been paid.

Moody will live a second life in sports as a head-coach: he will lead Boston College from 1943 to 1945 (11–7–1) and then Everett High School from 1955 to 1982—a record of 128–116–11 in 23 following years on the same bench.

CARLO SARNO

T
Holy Cross
1939 Providence Steamrollers (AA)
1940 Providence Steamrolers (AA)

In 1939 his team ranks second in the Northern Division and Sarno does his share.

GEORGE SAVARESE

HB
NYU
1938 Paterson Panthers—Union City Rams (AA)

A player in search for a protagonist role.

JOSEPH A. «JUMPIN' JOE» SAVOLDI   <u>**Born in Italy**</u>

FB
Notre Dame
1930 Chicago Bears (NFL)
Games:3; Rushing: 13, Yds 56; Avg 4,3, TD 1

Secret is his job.

The chronicles picture him as a native to Three Oaks, Michigan, but he was born in Milano (Italy) the 5th of March 1908.

In 1928 he arrives to Notre Dame; in his second year he leads the team in rushing, with 597 yards on 122 carries. In 1930 his career (possibly a shiny career) comes to an end at the third last game of the season because he has secretly married his girlfriend: the Catholic church was against secret marriages and Nothe Dame was a Catholic university; in October 1930 Notre Dame asks him to leave the campus. The Chicago Bears sign Savoldi straightaway, but his pro career will last only one season: the OSS (*Office of Strategic Services*) enrolls him.

After World War II, Savoldi will become a professional wrestler under the name of «The Mystery Man of World War II».

JOHNNY SCALZI

FB-RB
Georgetown
1931 Brooklyn Dodgers (NFL)
1931 Boston Braves (NL) <u>baseball team</u>
Games: 7; Passing: 7–16, Yds 96, TD 1; Punt Return: 3, Yds 35; Rushing 7, Yds 8.

In college times he plays 3 winning seasons (1928–30) with Georgetown. He is good also at baseball.

He will debut among the pros of both sports in the same years, but he will not do much in either of them (only 2 games on the diamond).

LARRY SCAROLA

FB-C
NYU
1938 Clifton Wessingtons (AA)

Part of an Italian-American colony (Zadra, Somma, Ventola, Fiore e Biritelli) whose general manager is called Fred Marchini, Scarola plays a weak and forgettable season.

ROCCO SCHIRALLI

G
Notre Dame
1939 East Chicago Indians (AFL)
1935 College All-Stars

Schiralli is engaged in the reborn AFL of 1939; the call arrives from the Chicago Indians sponsored by the Inland Steel Company. The season will end with a record of 4–3–0.

PASCHAL J. SCOTTINO

T
SMU
None
1935 SWC Champion
1936 East-West Shrine Game

He plays with the Mustangs from 1934 to 1936; in 1935 the team wins the conference title (record 12–1–0) and loses the *Rose Bowl* against Stanford; in the last year of college he will catch the eye of journalists and coaches and will be calles for the parade of end season

THOMAS A. «TONY» SIANO

C
Fordham
1932 Boston Braves (NFL)
1934 Brooklyn Dodgers (NFL)
Games: 20
1929 All-American

Siano, born in Massachussetts the son of a couple of immigrants, is the captain of Fordham for two years (1929–30).

In 1929 the Maroons win all the games of the season, and Siano is *All-American*. A journalist of *Associated Press*, stunned by the forbidding defense organized by Siano and friends (they will be scored only 3 TDs in the entire season), baptizes the line as *«The Seven Block of Granite»* (*see also* «Ed Franco»). The same line will be scored only 1 TD on rush in 1930, and Siano will be convoked to the *All-Stars Shrine East-West Game* set in San Francisco. For him the parade will repeat in 1931.

2 seasons and 20 honest games in NFL as a center.

JOSEPH «JOE» SOMMA

E
Broooklyn
1937 White Plains Bears (AA)
1937 Northern Division Champ
1937 AA Championship Game

A good rookie, a good team, a good season.

SAL SOMMA

QB-FB
NYU
1937 White Plains Bears (AA)
1938 Clifton Wessingtons (AA)

1937 Northern Division Champ
1937 AA Championship Game

A brotherly replay: a good rookie, a good team, a good season. But season two is played only to honor the contract.

VICTOR M. «VIC» SPADACCINI

FB-DB-WB
Minnesota
1938 Cleveland Rams (NFL)
1939 Cleveland Rams (NFL)
1940 Cleveland Rams (NFL)
1941 Columbus Bullies (AFL)
Games: 30; Receiving: 62, Yds 669, TD 3; Rushing: 9, Yds 47; PAT 17–23; Total Points 41
1938 College All-Stars
1941 AFL Champion

At the end of a good college career he plays in the Soldier's Field of Chicago before the 74,250 people audience of the game College All-Stars-Chicago Bears (final score: 39–20).

In his second year as a pro he will be the 4th best receiver of NFL. Before the end of his career, partly caused by his enrollment in World War II, he will conquer one AFL title with the Columbus Bullies.

AL SPINOSA

C
St.Vincent (Pa)
1937 Pittsburgh Americans (AFL)

A short and failing experience with a team that is disbanded in October, after only 3 games.

H. A. STELLA

T
Army
None
All-Time Army Players Squad

1936–1939 leading player. 1939 Captain.

FRANK STELLATELLA

G
Lafayette
None

As a rookie he is already the protagonist of the great 1937 season of Lafayette (record: 8–0–0).

MIKE STRAMIELLO

K-E-DE
Colgate
1930 Brooklyn Dodgers (NFL)
1931 Brooklyn Dodgers (NFL)
1932 Brooklyn Dodgers—Staten Islans Stapletons (NFL)
1934 Brooklyn Dodgers (NFL)
Games: 35 ; Receiving: 4, Yds 79; PAT 6/7; Punt 1, Yds 36
1930 NFL All-Pros

During a college football game in 1927, the forth quarter sees Colgate losing 6–9 against Syracuse.

Few minutes to go and it's Stramiello's turn to kick. Mike stops in the centre of the field, kneels down for a quick but heartfelt prayer, than goes on to kick the ball: 9–9 .

They talk about it in all the churches of the state.

During pro years he will defend more and kick less, confining himself to a precision job in the PATs.

In 1930 he will be included among the best players of the league. In the 1938 season he will land to the leadership of the Tonadoes: not a staggering experience.

ANDY TAMMARO

T-G
Richmond
1937 Brooklyn Bushwicks (AA)

An American Association rookie playing with the Brooklyn Bushwincks, the second new team of the league after the Eagles (formerly known as Brooklyn Bay Pakways).

BARRY TENORE

NB
?
1936 Mt. Vernon Cardinals (AA)

A light mark in the 1936 Cardinals team, alongside many other *paisà* (Fury DiMarzo, Patsy Egidio, Adolf Ausilio ...) Very few the information in the historical documents.

CARL A. TOMASELLO

DE
Scranton
1940 New York Giants (NFL)
1940–1941 Jersey City Giants (AA)
Games: 1
1939 All-American
1939 First Team All-State
1940 Blue&Gray Game

1940 College All-Stars Game
1940 AA Champion

A dominating player in his college years (in 1939 he was also the team captain), Tomasello is one of the best DE nationwide. Among the pros only a quick appearance in the NFL and a good season in the farm-team of Jersey City: he will also win the 1940 finals.

MARIO «MOTTS» TONELLI

FB-DB
Notre Dame
1940 Chicago Cardinals (NFL)
1945 Chicago Cardinals (NFL, he appeared briefly in one game only)
Games: 9 +1; Rushing: Rush 51, Yds 148, TD 1; Receiv.: Rec 5, Yds 53

His parents arrive from Northern Italy, and after the birth of Mario have settled in Chase Park, a borough of Chicago. At home sports were almost unknown and so the young Italian from the Windy City starts with the sports he first meets in catholic school: basketball and track. In High School he discovers organized football and becomes the school's star athlete. This will grant him easier studies: football might be a shortcut. His parents, though, disagree: sports are wasted time, not a respectable job. Mario instead dreams the beaches of California and the shirt of the USC Trojans.

When the time comes to choose the college, thunders and lightnings: «Not that far! Think of your mother!» Thanks God the second best choice is called Notre Dame (and coach Layden).

Tonelli becomes a star there, scoring a game-winning TD against USC (destiny at work …) and helping to lead the Fight to a national ranking. At the end of his college career Tonelli receives an offer as an assistant-coach and a promise to play as a pro: he signs a three years contract for 7,000 dollars a year. But after one season with the Cards, the war arrives onto him. Enrolled and bound to the Pacific, in the Philippines base of Clark Field; in 1942 he is one of the Americans soldiers who fight at Baatam and is captured by Japanese troops. He also takes part in the infamous Baatam Death March, seven days in hot tropical sun. Motts survives the terrifying march of over 60 miles with no water and his comrades falling around him. In America he is considered missing in action.

42 months later he is freed from a concentration camp in Japan by the American troops: he has endured the hunger, the sicknesses and all the harassments. In 1941 he weighed 212 pounds; when he is set free, he is 92.

As he will love to remember, «*When I came back, there was no celebration. My mother, dad, brother and sister and wife at the station. That was all*».

In the autumn of 1945 Charles Bidwill, the owner of the Cardinals will get to know that Tonelli misses only one game to be entitled to some pension: he will invite him to the training camp and after some practice he will put him on field for a quick official appearance.

Motts will find easily a way to re-enter civil life; after serving as Cook County's top environmental protection official he will retire in 1988.

AMERIGO «TONY» TONELLI

C-LB-G
USC
1939 Detroit Lions (NFL)
Games: 9

Only one season in NFL with the rebuilding Lions led by new coach Gus Henderson (6–5–0).

PAT TORTORELLA

E
Upsala
1937 Newark Tornadoes (AA)
1937 Southern Division Champ
1937 AA Championship Game

He plays only one season, picking a divisional title and reaching the league finales.

FRANCIS «BUD» TOSCANI

HB
St. Mary's
1932 Brooklyn Dodgers—Chicago Cardinals (NFL)
Games: 8

Two important seasons with St. Mary in 1930 (8–1–0, 10th in national ranking) and 1931 (8–2–0 and 3° rank).

He is a protagonist in the «Little Big Game», the challenge between the two major catholic schools of California.

In that period Santa Clara and St. Mary's had highly competitive teams. For the records, in 1934 Toscani completed 1 TD, and his college won 21–14.

FLAVIO J. «BULL» TOSI

E-DE
Boston College
1934 Boston Redskins (NFL)
1935 Boston Redskins (NFL)
1936 Boston Redskins (NFL)
Games: 27;Receiv. 17, 265 Yds, Avg 15,6, TD 2
1933 All-American,
1933 All-East Stars
Boston College Varsity Club Athletic Hall of Fame

He approaches football in the second half of the Twenties, in Beverly, MA; during high school he gains a reputation as a devastating tackle and a fierce fighter. The scouts of Boston College recruit him successfully: Flavio will be a star of the college, an outstanding pass receiver in offense but also a formidable defender.

In his college career many are the great episodes of his game, like the 10 sacks against the QB in one game; as a senior, he will be awarded All-America and All-East honors.

He will also be the first Boston College player to get to the NFL, signing with the Boston Redskins shortly after his degree.

Also in his pro years, Bull will go on playing with determination, deserving the respect of the champions of the league; at the end of one game, the great Bronko Nagurski of Chicago Bears will congratulate with him: «*I believe I was never hit as hard as today*».

His career will end before time because of a bad injury; he will then go back to his city, where he will work for the General Electric for 35 anni. He died aged 82 in 1994, leaving 5 sons.

Also for him the honour of appearing in the 1935 Nat. Chicles cards.

JOSEPH «JOHN» TOSI

C-LB-T
Niagara
1939 Pittsburgh Pirates—Brooklyn Dodgers (NFL)
Games: 4

In his one year as a pro, big John Tosi (225 pounds) opens the season in Pittsburgh, a «country-club friends» sort of team, not very keen on quality agonism; the change of Head-Coach will not save the last part of the season (1–9–1). Tosi will close it in Brooklyn with the Dodgers, like his teammate Dick Nardi.

ANGELO TRENTO

G
Syracuse
None.

1934 starter at Syracuse University.

MIKE TURCONE

C
Brown
1938 Union City Rams (AA)

One year in the American with the farm-team of the Brooklyn Dodgers.

DOMINIC M. «DOM» VAIRO

E-DE
Notre Dame
1935 Green Bay Packers (NFL)
Games : 1

Captain of the Irish in 1934 (6–3–0). In 1935 he ranks 2nd in the NFL Western Division with the Packers of Curly Lambeau, closed in a corner by a guy named Don Hutson.

FRED G. «CHOPPER» VANZO

BB-LB
Northwestwern
1938 Detroit Lions (NFL)
1939 Detroit Lions (NFL)
1940 Detroit Lions (NFL)
1941 Detroit Lions—Chicago Cardinals (NFL)
Games: 39; Rushing 6, 45 Yds; Receiving 17, 257 Yds
1938 College All-Stars

A valuable player in college, selected for the 1938 College All-Stars team and pro-tagonist of the victory against the Chicago Bears. Vanzo will be chosen by the NY Giants at the 2nd round of the 1938 draft, but he will play four years as a pro in Detroit. The only dazzling feature is the weight: in 1938–1939 he was 230 pounds, the heaviest of his team and, together with Armand Niccolai (230), of the whole NFL.

For the record, second heaviest was another *paisà*: Vic Spadaccini, 225 pounds. In 1940 the new number one of this peculiar list will be George Somers, a tackle of Philadelphia Eagles weighing a formidable (at least for the times) 260 pounds!

GEORGE VENEROSO

T
Temple
1938 Wilmington Clippers (AA-Independent)
1939 Wilmington Clippers (AA)
1940 Wilmington Clippers (AA)

Plays in the team managed by Sam DeLuca; a three years adventure paying 1 TD.

ARMANDO «BURST» VENTOLA

G
Temple
1936 Orange Tornadoes (EFL)
1937 Newark Tornadoes (EFL)
1938 Clifton Wessington (EFL)

He is always the biggest (and largest) player of his team. He has to bear the cross.

FRED VENTURELLI

G-T
None
1939 Kenosha Cardinals (AFL)

21 years old Fred, 230 pounds and little schooling, fights his battles at Lake Front Stadium; an idol for the supporters.

MIKE «SUNSHINE» VETRANO

C
NYU
1936 Mt. Vernon Cardinals (AA)

Vetrano is the biggest of the team: 225 pounds.

VICTOR J. «PUTT» VIDONI

E
Duquesne
1935 Pittsburgh Pirates (NFL)
1936 Pittsburgh Pirates (NFL)
Games: 13; Rec. 13, yards 146

In 1933 he is a regular at Duquesne together with the others *paisà* DeLuca, Ciccone, Niccolai and Zaninelli; the team ends the seasn with a 10–1–0 record (13th in the national ranking). Curiously, his pro experience (2 seasons with the Pirates) takes place with the same 3 teammates he played with at college.

DICK VITULLO

HB
Providence
1938 Jersey City Giants (AA)
1939 Providence Steamrollers (AA)
1938 AA Title

In 1938 he is the champion of the league with teh team managed by Tim Mara. The following season Vitullo contributes to the second ranik in the division.

STEVE «SPARKY» ZADRA

C-G
Knox
1936 Passaic Red Devils (AA)
1937 Brooklyn Eagles (AA)

In 1936 he is the defensive hound of Eddie Turecki, the Red Devils QB. In 1937 he signs for the Brooklyn Eagles, that end their season in the Southern Division with a 4–3–1. In 1938 he follows QB Turecki to Clifton: a season to forget.

SILVIO ZANINELLI

BB-FB-DB
Duquesne
1934 Pittsburgh Pirates (NFL)
1935 Pittsburgh Piartes (NFL)
1936 Pittsburgh Pirates (NFL)
1937 Pittsburgh Pirates (NFL)
Games: 44; Rushing 81, Yds 150, TD 1; Receiving 7, Yds 41; Pass 15,2.

1933 starter fullback at Duquesne. With the Dukes he plays an important season (significant victories against West Virginia, Detroit, Westminster, Washington and Jefferson) ending with the controversy about an invitation game in Florida. The *Palm Festival* (bound to become in 1935 the *Orange Bowl*) will register a sound 33–7 victory against Miami, FL.

Zaninelli will play 4 years in the NFL Pirates team of Art Rooney; his best year will be that of 1936 (61 carries and 2 receivings), with the Pirates ranking 2nd in the East Division (6–6–0).

FRANK ZOPPETTI

QB-DB
Duquesne
1941 Pittsburgh Steelers (NFL)
Games: 4; Pass 1–0

1936 Orange Bowl
Duquesne All-Time Team

In 1936 he leads the Dukes to yet another winning season (8–2–0, 14th in National Rank); prestigious victories (14–0 against Rice, 7–0 against Pittsburgh, 33–0 against Geneva, 13–0 against Carnegie Tech and 26–0 against Washington)—how many adversaries left with a 0 on the scoreboard!

At the end of the season, a breathless game against Mississippi State gives Zappetti and Co. One of the first editions of a prestigious Bowl.

In 1941 Buff Donelli will call him to Pittsburgh, but the experience will not be a lucky one.

THE FORTIES

BACKDROP

In 1940 George Halas leads the Chicago Bears to the NFL Championship Game against the Washington Redskins and his «Monsters of the Bay» win with a devastating 73–0. On the field **Maniaci** e **Famiglietti** leave their mark on the scoring: the first running to touchdown for 42 yards and then adding a PAT, the latter with another touchdown in a 2 yards run.

On the 8th of October Maryland plays against Pennsylvania in the first TV broadcast college football game ever; the year before NBC had already aired a training session of Fordham. The winner of the 1940 Heisman Trophy Tom Harmon (halfback for Michigan) is the strongest college player of these years, kept under observation by the major pro teams. After Pearl Harbour he asks to serve under the army; during an air transfer he will be the only survivor in the crash of his plane; he will jump with his parachute and will be intercepted by Japanese soldiers; Chinese partisans will rescue him. After the end of the war he will get back to Michigan to marry a famous actress and model who will wear for the ceremony a dress made with the hero's parachute. Harmon will then return to pro football playing for the Los Angeles Rams, reemploying himself at the end of his career as a commentator for the new successful medium: TV.

A third *American Football League* starts, only to disappear in a couple of years.

A network of 120 radio stations airs the championship throughout the States, reaching the remotest corners of the nation.

In 1941 the NFL publishes its first official Record Manual; the NCAA introduces the free player substitutions. The AFL plays its last season, although it will still have some future. On 7th of December, during the interval of a game, at the Polo Grounds of New York the loudspeakers transmit an urgent message: «*All armed forces personnel are requested to report to their commands immediately ... Repeat ...* "

The Japanese have attacked.

On the 6th of December only 13,341 people are in Chicago for the NFL Championship Game. In 1942 many players are on their way to the war service, while some veterans in disarm get back on the playing fields. By the end of the hostilities there will be 638 NFL athletes at the front, 355 in the second lines, 16 decorated and 21 dead in combat.

In 1943 **Angelo Bertelli** wins the Heisman Trophy; he is the first paisà to a «graduate» in college football.

In 1945 Cecil Isbell of Purdue is the first coach to guide his team from the press tribune in order to get a wider vision of the field and of the movements of his athletes.

In 1946 Wake Forest confronts South Carolina in the first edition of the *Gator Bowl*, disputed in Jacksonville, Florida. Arch Ward, a sports editor for the *Chicago Tribune,* organizes a new pro league understanding the hunger of Americans for sports news after the wartime.

George Connor of Notre Dame wins the first edition of the *Outland Award*, assigned by the *Football Writers Association of America* to the outstanding interior lineman of the year.

In 1947 Orlando hosts the first *Tangerine Bowl*; in 1983 the game will be renamed as the *Florida Citrus Bowl.*

In 1948 the Cleveland Browns win their third AAFC (*All-American Football Conference*) title in a row. Also in 1948 the Rams appear on the field wearing helmets painted with their logo: it is the first time.

In 1949 the NFL merges with the AAFC, absorbing 3 new teams: Cleveland Browns, San Francisco 49ers and Baltimore Colts. In the same year debuts an athlete named **Taliaferro**, a surname apparently Italian («Tagliaferro» or «Tagliaferri» meaning originally «ironcutter»). Actually, this Taliaferro is called George and is the first afro-american player to be chosen in an NFL draft.

Ted Nugent, head coach at Virginia Military Institute, introduces the «I formation», wich features all the running backs lined up in a row behind the quarterback; the new formation gains fame when used by Frank Leahy at Notre Dame a few years later. In the closing decade also played thre Italian-Americans bound to get into the *Pro Football Hall of Fame:* **Canadeo, Lavelli** and **Trippi**. *The Hall of Fame Selection Committee,* will also include in the *All-Pro Squad of the 1940s* **Ferrante** and **Banducci**, the latter being the only one born in Italy.

With the arrival of the Fifties, football is ready to challenge baseball on the grounds of popularity.

In the *Canadian Football League* **Pat Santucci** is one of the winners of the *Grey Cup* of 1943, 1945 and 1946; **Ollie Segatori** will follow his example in 1949 with the Montreal Alouettes.

THE NAMES

LOUIS J. «DUKE» ABBRUZZI

HB-DB
Rhode Island
1941 Providence Steamrollors (AA)-Churchill Pros (Independent)
1946 Boston Yanks (NFL)
Games:3; Rushing 6, yards 26; Rec, 2, yards 55; KR 8, yards 147 (NFL);
Rhode Island Athletic Hall of Fame
Warren Hall of Fame
Providence Gridiron Club Hall of Fame

A brilliant college career, All-England in football for 3 years and All-East in 1941. Captain of the teams of all the 3 sports (football, baseball, basketball). After a short experience in the American Association (counting 5 TDs in the season) he played professionally in the Baseball Colonial League and with the Boston Yanks in NFL.

Later he became a good teacher and coach in different schools (DeLaSalle Academy, Rogers-Thompson High, Newport), winning also a State title in 1971.

ANGELO ACOCELLA

T
Syracuse
None

1945 team captain at Syracuse. Takes part to the 1947 *Shrine East-West Game*.

ANTHONY S. «TONY» AIELLO

WB-FB
Youngstown St.
1944 Detroit Lions—Brooklyn Tigers (AFL)
Games : 5; Rush: 6, 22yards; KR 1, 9 yards
YSU Hall of Fame

Four games with Detroit together with the great Frankie Sinkwich and one game on the East Coast, at Brooklyn, in a definitely losing team still under reconstruction.

GASPER AMMENDOLIA

G
Northeastern
None

After the war, in 1946 he is on the field with the Bears (3–3–0).

A few quality games before he abandons the studies.

THOMAS «TOM» ALBERGHINI

G
Holy Cross
1945 Pittsburgh Steelers (NFL)
Games: 1

One single game in a team with many troubles, another season thrown away (2–8–0).

VITO F. ANANIS

HB
Boston College
1940 Providence Steamrollers (AA)-Boston Bears (AFL)

1941 Churchill Pros (Independent-AA)
1942 Worcester Panthers (AA)
1945 Washington Redskins (NFL)
Games: 1; Rushing: 3, 8 yards (NFL); Rec.: 7, 118 yards; 13 Points (AFL)
1939 All-East;
1939 All-American;
1940 College All-Star Team;
Boston College Varsity Club Athletic Hall of Fame.

French-Italian by origins, in 1939 he was a key player at Boston College, conquering some prestigious sports titles; during his senior year he was a very productive runner (12 TDs) who contributed to his team's first post-season apparition: the 1940 Cotton Bowl.

In the same year he is on the field with the College All-Stars, winning the game against the New York Giants pro team.

Not many his experiences as a pro: the first ones at the beginning of the Forties, the last one by the half of the decade. In between, the war.

After his playing experiences hi will begin a coaching career in the secondary school. It will prove a long and lucky job.

ALBERT F. «AL» BAISI

G
West Virginia
1940 Chicago Bears (NFL)
1941 Chicago Bears (NFL)
1946 Chicago Bears (NFL)
1947 Philadelphia Eagles (NFL)
Games: 22
1940 NFL Champion
1941 NFL Champion
1946 NFL Champion
1947 Eastern Division Title
1947 NFL Championship Game

After the end of a positive experience in college, Baisi debuts with the Bears in the 1940 season.

8–3–0 in regular season, a sound victory at the Championship Game (Chicago smashes Washington 73–0). 1941 is also a lucky year for him: the Bears win the Western Division (10–1–0) and then the Championship Game (37–9 against the NY Giants).

At the beginning of the war, Baisi goes on to fight for his country; he will be back on the fields 4 years later.

By the end of the war the Americans are eager to get immediately back to a normal life, with no cables from the Defense, no war bonds, no rationings. The Bears do their job in full, calling back the champions of 1940–1941 like Baisi, offering a good level football, getting important victories and, again, vast audiences to the stadiums. The season of 1946 is marked by yet another NFL Championship won (Bears-NY Giants 24–14).

Al Baisi spends the last «coins» of his successful career playing for the Eagles, a strong and winning teamthat will gain the division title.

With Philadelphia Baisi will also dispute the NFL Championship Game against the Cardinals. It will end with a small measure defeat (Chicago Cardinals-Philadelphia Eagles 28–21), decided by a 70 yards run to TD by Elmer Angsman.

Once retired he will work as a manager of public venues. The last one, the «Alary's Bar» run together with his son is a paradise for Bears fans in Minnesota. On the wall, a neon ad of a famous Italian beer side by side with a full-size photograph of Baisi himself. More photos are on the other walls. In the bar the talk is mostly football.

EDWARD T. «ED» BALATTI

E-DB
None
1946 S.Francisco 49ers (AAFC)
1947 S.Francisco 49ers (AAFC)
1948 S.Francisco 49ers-New York Yankees-Buffalo Bills (AAFC)

Games: 38; Rec. 12, 113 yards, 1 TD; Punt Return 2, 8 yards, 1 TD; Int.1, 1 TD;
XP 3–3; Points 21
1948 AAFC Championship Game

Balatti debuts among the pros with a franchise organised by Tony Morabito in the new AAFC league. He will play alongside Banducci (newly arrived from the Eagles) in a winning season (9–5–0, second ranking in the division behind the superchampions Browns). The same story in 1947: winning season (8–4–2) and second ranking after Cleveland; Balatti is one of the targets of QB Frankie Albert, together with Alyn Beals.

A complicated 1948, marked by sudden team changes, ends his career.

BRUNO BANDUCCI   Born in Italy

OG-DG
Stanford
1944 Philadelphia Eagles (NFL)
1945 Philadelphia Eagles (NFL)
1946 S.Francisco 49ers (AAFC)
1947 S.Francisco 49ers (AAFC)
1948 S.Francisco 49ers (AAFC)
1949 S.Francisco 49ers (AAFC)
1950 S.Francisco 49ers (NFL)
1951 S.Francisco 49ers (NFL)
1952 S.Francisco 49ers (NFL)
1953 S.Francisco 49ers (NFL)
1954 S.Francisco 49ers (NFL)
1955–56 Toronto Argonauts (CFL)
Games: 78   Points 6 (NFL Stats)
1944 College All-Star
1947 AAFC All-League team
1949 AAFC Final Championship
1953,1954 NFL All-Pro
The Hall of Fame Committee 1940's All-ProTeam.

Banducci, born on the 16th of November of 1920 in «Tasignano» (i.e. Tassignano,Tuscany, Italy), after a good college career culminating with the selection fot the 1944 edition of the College All-Stars, lands to NFL called by the Philadelphia Eagles; in team lead by Grease Nealy (a qualified coach pretty well-known in the world of football) he puts himself under a good light although being part of a line packed full of big names. On the East Coast Banducci plays with quality in a winning group which ranks second in the conference chart for two years in a row, two years of fights to open a breach tc the formidable Steve Van Buren, NFL best runner of 1945.The programs and the money of a new league, the AAFC, persuade Bruno to move to California. New coach Buck Shaw entrusts to him the leadership of the offensive line of the 49ers: his first priority will be sustaining the job of top runner Norm Staudler (another redux from NFL).

Bruno will play with the 49ers for 9 seasons (8 of which winning seasons), always as a regular, always gathering honur, fame, good contracts.

In 1947 he is an All-League Team as AAFC best player in his role; in 1949 he will dispute the finals of the league.

When NFL absorbs AAFC, three new teams will add to the major league: San Francisco 49ers, Baltimore Colts and Cleveland Browns.

Once returned to NFL Banducci will belie all kind of detractors, who sustained that the new league was way less competitive. In this he will also be helped by the team of Cleveland: the Browns will dominate NFL for many years, and he will be All-Pro for 2 years in a row. Facts instead of words.

Before storing the shoes down the cellar, he will still spend two years in Canada, playing for the Toronto team.At the end of the Fifties we find him again on the sideline of the Eagles, as an assistant coach this time.

ANDY BARBIERI

G-T
NYU
1940 Long Island Indians (AA)
1941 Long Island Indians (AA)-Churchill Pros (Independent)

Barbieri debuts in the Detroit Lions farm club, playing some games.

VINCE BARTOLOMEO

QB
Penn Military
1946 Wilmington Clippers (AFL)

He is a QB under observation of the Washington Redskins coaching staff. They decide to use the Clippers as a trial bench. 1946 will not be a great season (1–7–2).

FRANK BASILE

HB-DB
West Chester State
1948 Wilmington Clippers (AFL)
1949 Wilmington Clippers (AFL)
1948 AFL Playoffs
1948 AFL Championship Game
1949 AFL Playoffs

A good athlete realising 5 intercepts in the 1948 regular season. He reaches the AFL finals, where he scores 1 TD after recovering a fumble.

In 1949 he does even better, realising 6 intercepts for a total 100 yards.

P. BELLANI

G
St. Mary
None

He is a 1942 All-American Blockers (a «Chattanooga Times» selection).

LOU BELLINA

T
None
1949 Jersey City Giants (AFL)

A barely visible mark in AFL.

JOE BERARDELLI

T
Ohio State
1940 Newark Bears (AA)
1941 Newark Bears (AA)
1942 Wilmington Clippers (AA)
1940 AA Playoffs

A good athlete in the farm club of the Chicago Bears.

DOM «BLAKIE» BERARDUCCI

B
None
1949 Erie Vets (AFL-Independent)

Blakie plays in a team disputing some games against some of the biggest franchises of the AFL. The Vets exist since 1946, when they gave life to a semipro team playing games outside the organised championships.

LIBERO «LIBBY» BERTAGNOLLI

G-LB
Washington (St.Louis)
1939 St.Louis Gunners (AFL)
1940 St. Louis Gunners (AFL)-Phoenix Panthers (PCFL)
1942 Chicago Cardinals (NFL)

1945 Chicago Cardinals (NFL)
Games: 11 (NFL)

Libby debuts among the pros with an AFL team in a season complicated by the frequent change of coaches and managers. Anyway he plays his role, that of a careful and reliable guard.

In 1940 he plays in another minor, battling on the fields of the *Pacific Coast Football League* with an Arizona team.

In 1942 arrives the call from the Cardinals: Bertagnolli will play 11 out of 12 games with them; the season of the boys of Conzelman is not peculiarly brilliant also because of the calls of duty of the Army, depriving of some of their best athletes. Also Bertagnolli will serve the Countru in 1943–1944.

He will get back to the NFL in 45, in a championship and a team way different: new players, new schemes (the Cardinals too will adopt the T-formation). Hard times for the vets, and Libby will play only one game.

ANGELO BORTOLO BERTELLI

QB
Notre Dame
1946–48, Los Angeles Dons (AAFC)
College stats: Games: 26; Passing: 167–318, 2.578 yards, 28 TDs pass.
Pro: Passing 76–166, 970 yards; 7 TDs pass
1942, 1943 All-American;
COLLEGE HALL OF FAME.

Bertelli, son of emigrants, has been one of the big protagonists of college football; «The Arm» or «The Springfield Rifle» or also «Mr. Accuracy», he has been a really polyvalent athlete, a best player of football, baseball and hockey, boasting many All-America nominations. In 1941, in the lead of Notre Dame, he completes passages for 1027 yards, ranking number two in the Heisman Trophy rush. In 1942 he plays another high level season, taking the best from coach Leahy's new T-Formation schemes; in 1943 he leads the team to the national title and obtains the Heisman Trophy, just before being called to the Army in the Navy and leaving to serve in the Pacific. In the meanwhile, the best journalists of the country write articles about him full of compliments and rich with enthusiastic critics. On his return from the war, after some decorations deserved in Guam, he gets back to football, signing for the Los Angeles Dons, one of the pro teams of the new *All-America Football Conference* (AAFC). It will prove as a short and not significant experience, marked by a major injury which will stop his career. The new league, one of the many trying to escape the monopoly of NFL, will play only few seasons and then will be absorbed into the major league. One of its team, the Cleveland Browns, will mark an era of the sport (three finals in a row in AAFC, the same in NFL). Bertelli has lived for 48 years in the small city of Clifton, NJ, trading in beer and spirits; together with wife Gilda Passerini has sponsored some local teams which eventually launched such players as Nick Buoniconti and Joe Scibelli, landed to NFL. A quiet life, a nice family, many stories to tell a at the parties, at the pub, in the best drawing room.»*One day my daughter Laureen, the eldest of my children, brought home his boyfriend. The boy saw my Heisman Trophy in the glass cabinet and asked my daughter for some information. Well, he spent the night talking with me. Paying no attention at all to Laureen and the rest of the family.*»

Angelo has always declared not to be the extraordinary player everybody wanted to see, only a lucky boy who had the chance of being at the right place in the right time. The calm of the strong.

GERALD BERTUCCI

G
LSU
None
1944 All-SEC Team

One of the best guards of 1944 in the whole conference.

JOHN BINOTTO

FB
Duquesne
None

In 1949 he is one of the best players of Duquesne

LEN BONFORTE

HB-DB
Georgetown
1948 Bethlehem Bulldogs (AFL)
1949 Bethlehem Bulldogs (AFL)
1949 AFL Playoffs

In 1948 he performs 4 intercepts for a total 49 yards. The Bulldogs are 1 of the 6 teams playing that year in the AFL, where the divisions have been eliminated and resists a single grouping subject to some new rules: roster limit of 22 players; salary cap at $ 2,000 a game per team. In 1949 Bonforte scores the only TD of the team during the playoffs (pass by Ray Dini).

ERNEST B. «ERNIE» BONELLI

FB-LB-HB-DB
Pittsburgh
1945 Chicago Cardinals (NFL)
1946 Pittsburgh Steelers (NFL)
Games: 10; Rush. 38, 100 yards; Rec. 4, 35 yards; PR. 3, 37 yards ; KR. 2, 45 yards ; 4 Fumbles.
1945 Blue-Gray All-Stars Game
1945 College All-Stars
All-American Football Third Air Force II WW
Pennsylvania Sports Hall of Fame
2004 FC Hall of Fame.

A very good player in High School during the second half of the 30s, Bonelli lands to Pittsburgh University to play both football and baseball with great results.

In the course of World War II we find him fighting in North Africa, where he will deserve seven battle ribbons.

After the war Bonelli will play for two years as an NFL pro. His engagement will be of 400 dollars per game: not so bad for the 40s. Once retired he will become a medical products retailer, living in Pittsburgh before moving to Florida: 3 days a week playing golf and the rest training young players. In the May of 2004, at the age of 85, he will be included in the Hall of Fame of his High School. An amazing 75 years back jump ...

VICTOR «VIC» BONFILI

HB-OE
West Virginia
None
1948 Sun Bowl

A good college career culminating in 1948 with a brilliant season: 535 yards run and 24 passes caught for 244 more.

The Mountaineers, also thanks to him, will win the *Sun Bowl* against Texas-El Paso for 21–12.

ANTHONY J. «TONY» BOVA

E-DB-DE-QB
St. Francis
1942 Pittsburgh Steelers (NFL)
1943 Philadelphia Eagles-Pittsburgh Steelers (NFL)
1944 Chicago Cardinals-Pittsburgh Steelers (NFL)
1945 Pittsburgh Steelers (NFL)
1946 Pittsburgh Steelers (NFL)
1947 Pittsburgh Steelers (NFL)
Games: 61; Rec. 60, 1,129 yards, 7 TDs; KR. 3, 42 yards

Bova lands to NFL in a team full of Italian-Americans: Niccolai, Donelli, Cherundolo, Binotto; during the first year Bova is a sort of a factotum: defending, returning, receiving ... The team ends the season second in the division with a record of 7–4–0. 1943 is a difficult year and the teams of Philadelphia and Pittsburgh decide to merge for economic reasons. For Bova it will be the chance to gain the spotlight and complete 17 receivings and 5 TDs. In 1944 comes another temporary merger, this time with the Cardinals; Tony will be their second QB and a not so incisive runner.

In the three years from 1945 to 1947 the Steelers are back as an independent team, marking a constant innuendo in the NFL championship (2–8–0 in 1945, 5–5–1 the following year and 8–4–0 in 1947). In his last year as a pro Bova will be displayed as a defensive end and will contribute to the good season of the team, ranking second in the division.

PAUL BROGLIO

G
Ohio State
1949 Wilmington Clippers (AFL)

A good college experience, a short seasonal experience in the AFL.

PAUL BRUNO

G
West Chester State
1946 Wilmington Clippers (AFL)

A quick passage in a minor league.

AMEDEO R. «MIKE» BUCCHIANERI

G
Indiana
1941 Wilmington Clippers (AA)
1941 Green Bay Packers (NFL)
1942 Wilmington Clippers (AA)
1944 Green Bay Packers (NFL)
1945 Green Bay Packers (NFL)
Games: 14
1941 College All-Stars

1944 NFL Western Division Title
1944 NFL Champion

A good prospect in High School, Bucchinaeri gains the spotlight in 1937. Then, from 1938 to 1940, he plays for the Indiana University.

He becomes a pro in 1941 with the Packers, a 10–1–0 team led by Curly Lambeau that will rank 2nd in the Western Division.

After a two years break (with a quick passage in the American Association), Amedeo is back on the field in the autumn of 1944.

In this season the Packers are a well structured team, with the right mix of veterans in great shape and young players of clear talent: they will win the divisional title and the NFL Championship Game (14–7 against the NY Giants). The following year the Packers and Bucchianeri will not repeat the season of 1944, also because of the retirement of some great players. And for Amedeo too is time to store away the playing shoes.

L. C. BUFALINO

QB
Cornell
None

1941 leading passer.

LAWRENCE A. «LARRY» CABRELLI

E-DE-DB
Colgate
1941 Philadelphia Eagles (NFL)
1942 Philadelphia Eagles (NFL)
1943 Philadelphia Eagles-Pittsburgh Steelers (NFL)
1944 Philadelphia Eagles (NFL)
1945 Philadelphia Eagles (NFL)
1946 Philadelphia Eagles (NFL)

1947 Philadelphia Eagles (NFL)
Games: 61; Rec. 68, 925 Yds., 5 TDs ; KR. 2, 25 Yds.
1947 NFL Western Division Title
1947 NFL Championship Game

A whole career with the Eagles. In his first NFL year he receives 4 times totalling 90 yards and 1 TD. In 1942 Cabrelli is the best receiver with a record of 15 receivings, 229 yards and 1 TD. He will repeat himself in 1943, with 199 yards and another 1 TD. In 1944 the Eagles climb back the chart with a winning record, at last (7–1–2), and Larry is once again the best receiver of the team (14 rec., 169 yards, 1 TD). The following year he is again the second best target (8 rec., 190 yards) for Tommy Thompson, the one-eyed QB.

In 1946 Cabrelli is still a trustworthy athlete of coach Greasy Neale and goes on catching flying balls with good continuity (8 rec., 98 yards, 1 TD). Meanwhile, his team goes on being the second force of the division. The twilight of Cabrelli arrives when the Eagles reach the top of the chart, but he still manages to become a reliable defensive end, able to pick the last, important rewards. Not too lucky his partecipation to the NFL Championship Game of the 28th of December: the Eagles are beaten 28–21 by the Chicago Cardinals.

RALPH C. CALCAGNI

T
Pennsylvania
1946 Boston Yanks (NFL)
1947 Pittsburgh Steelers (NFL)
Games: 20; 2 Points

Coming from the Quakers and the Ivy League, he plays as a pro with the Boston team of Ted Collins, in a «heap» of paisà (Governali, Famiglietti, Canale, Abbruzzi, Romboli, Zeno) some of which are only rookies.

Big audience (50,000 fans in home games), meager results.

In 1947 he passes to the Steelers led by Jock Sutherland, ranking second in the Eastern Division with a 8–4–0 record.

PETE CALCAGNO

C
Bucknell
1946 Newark Bombers (AFL)
1948 Newark Bears (AFL-Independent)

One season and a half in a not exactly winning team for a discrete center. In 1948 the team of Newark will stop playing after 4 games.

JOHNNY CALCATERRA

HB
Connecticut
1941 Hartford Blues (Independent)

Plays for an independet team scoring 4 points with the PATs

LEONARD J. «LEN» CALLIGARO

FB-LB-QB
Wisconsin
1944 New York Giants (NFL)
1946 Jersey City Giants (AFL)
1947 Jersey City Giants (AFL)
Games: 10; Rush 3, 4 yards, 1 TD; Rec. 2, 11 yards; 6 Points(NFL)
1944 NFL Eastern Division Title
1944 NFL Championship Game
1946 AFL Divisional Title
1946 AFL Champion

After arriving 3rd in the national ranking with the Badgers in 1942, Calligaro knows one single important season in the NFL. He diputes all the games (he is 23 years old) but is overwhelmed by runners much stronger and with more experience than him. The team wins the division title and on the 17th of December 1944 disputes the NFL Championship Game, losing against the Green Bay Packers. In 1946 we find him in the farm team of the Giants, playing the role of QB and winning the league. In 1947 we find him among the best receivers of the AFL .

ANTHONY T. «TONY» CALVELLI

C-LB-G
Stanford
1939 Detroit Lions (NFL)
1940 Detroit Lions (NFL)
Games : 18 ; Int. 2, 51 yards, 1 TD

Calvelli arrives to NFL to play in a team which is losing all the champions who made it great in the 30s (Dutch Clark, George Christensen, Ace Gutowski, Ernie Caddel).

Also the second year is complicated for Tony, with the management of the Lions divided and quarrelling; still he will play 11 games, protagonist of a couple of intercepts, one of which completed in end zone.

NICHOLAS W. «NICK» CAMPOFREDA

C-T
Western Maryland
1944 Washington Redskins (NFL)
Games: 3

He arrives late to the NFL, aged 30. A quick and heavy passage: with his 240lb he is a giant in the team.

ANTHONY R. «TONY» CANADEO

HB-DB-FB
Gonzaga
1941 Green Bay Packers (NFL)
1942 Green Bay Packers (NFL)
1943 Green Bay Packers (NFL)

1944 Green Bay Packers (NFL)
1946 Green Bay Packers (NFL)
1947 Green Bay Packers (NFL)
1948 Green Bay Packers (NFL)
1949 Green Bay Packers (NFL)
1950 Green Bay Packers (NFL)
1951 Green Bay Packers (NFL)
1952 Green Bay Packers (NFL)
Games: 116; Rushing: 1,025, 4,127 yards, 26 TDs; Rec.: 69, 579 yards, 5 TDs;
Passing: 105–268, yards 1,642; TDs pass 16; Punting: 45, 1,669 yards; Punt Ret.:
51, 585 yards; KickRet.: 80, 1,887 yards; Total Points: 186
1939 All-American
1943 NFL All-Pro
1944 NFL Western Division Title
1949 NFL All-Pro
NFL ALL-PROS 40s
NAIA Hall of Fame
Wisconsin Hall of Fame
Packers Ironmen Era All-Time Team
PRO FOOTBALL HALL OF FAME

One of the biggest players of all times for the Packers, coming from Gonzaga, where he had been an All-America in 1939. «The Grey Ghost» will play for 11 years at Green Bay, the most difficult years for the team, with a constant render. Very determined and versatile (a runner, a returner, a kicker, a receiver and also a passer) he will have an average income of 25 yards per game all along his career. Averaged 75 yards all categories in 116 games!!

He always played at the highest levels, even in the worst seasons for his team, as when in 1949 the Packers ranked last in their division even if he had run over 1,000 yards (he is the third athlete in the history of NFL to cross this limit).

Some milestones:

1942, he is the best runner of the league;
1943, he is selected for the All-Pro;
1946, he is among the 5 top runners;
1949, he is All-Pro again.

Among the many acknowledgements, also the inclusion in the ideal team of the 40s as a regular.

In 1945 he took part to World War II.

EMILIO «EMILE» CANALE

T
Upsala
1948 Paterson Panthers (AFL)
1948 AFL Playoffs
1948 AFL Champion

A good player who will arrive to the title of the league in one single season.

ROCCO P. «WALKING BILLBOARD» CANALE

T-G
Boston College
1943 Philaldelphia Eagles-Pittsburgh Steelers (NFL)
1944 Philadelphia Eagles (NFL)
1945 Philadelphia Eagles (NFL)
1946 Boston Yanks (NFL)
1947 Boston Yanks (NFL)
Games: 38
1941 Sugar Bowl
1942 All-East
1943 All-American
1943 Orange Bowl
Boston College Varsity Club AthleticHall of Fame

For him a shiny career in the college football, summing up 26 victories out of 31 games disputed. Canale dominates both as an offensive lineman and as a defensive lineman. His extraordinary skill in blocking and tackling make him a key element for his team.

Chosen by Philadelphia, le arrives among the pros full of expectations.

The times are not so good: the financial and athletic poverty (with some of the best players busy with the war) obliges the franchises of Philadelphia and Pittsburgh to join their forces and organize a patchwork selection that will anyway win 5 games out of 10.

The following year the Eagles are back as an independent team and Canale and friends are running for the divisional title and end 2nd at the last moment with a record of 7–1–2, showing some individualities of all respect. Same story in 1945 (7–3–0), with a Canale not much used because of some injuries.

In 1946 comes a change of team: Rocco, aged 29 for 253 lbs. (the Maciste of the group), becomes the «nurse» of the franchise organized by Ted Collins. Hard times and full arenas (record: 2–8–1), with a young and skilled QB to protect: Paul Governali.

1947 his is last year as a pro: he will dispute 10 games out of 12. The results of the Yanks are neatly improving, also thanks to the the arrival of a new willing coach, and the team ranks 3rd in the division. The career of Rocco was a good career, hailed with favour by the Eastern press.

VINCE CANTINI

QB
Carneige Tech

The best passer of 1941.

PHIL CANTORE

QB-FB
South Carolina
1948 Paterson Panthers (AFL)
1949 Paterson Panthers (AFL)
1948 AFL Playoffs
1948 AFL Title
1949 AFL Playoffs
1949 AFL Championship Game

The successes of the team in 1948 come with Cantore as Allie Sherman's back-up. The following year he will be used also as a FB and will realise 3 TDs.

ROLAND CARANCI

T
Colorado
1944 New York Giants (NFL)
Games:2
1943 Mountain States Conference Title
1944 Eastern Division Title

Toccata e fuga …

Only 2 presences for Roland, with the Giants that win the Eastern Division and dispute the NFL Championship Game against the Packers, losing it.

VINCENT «VIN» CARLESIMO

G-T
Villanova
1946 Newark Bombers-Paterson Panthers (AFL)
1948 Newark Bears (AFL-Independent)

Carlesimo plays in a minor league with 2 different teams, one of which organized by the Newark Club together with the Chicago Bears.

JOSEPH «JOE» CARLO

T
None
1946 Scranton Miners (AFL)

A former miner sometimes towering (280 lbs) over the lines.

AL CARUSO

QB-E
Manhattan
1940 Jersey City Giants (AA)
1941 Jersey City Giants (AA)
1940 AA Title
1941 AA Playoffs

In his first year in the American Association he finds a place in the team as a receiver, playing 5 games with a record of 5 for 73 yards. The direction of the game is still in the hands of Danowski and Caruso will have to wait until 1941 to play as a QB. Then he will show a good game, completing 2 TDs.

RICHARD P. «DICK» CASSIANO

T-HB-DB
Pittsburgh
1940 Brooklyn Dodgers (NFL)
Games: 10; Passing 9–30, 128 yards, 1TD; Rush.:35, yards 84; Rec. 2, yards 67, TDs 2

In his college years he plays in the last Panthers team (the «dream backfield»). A single season playing all the roles with the team led by a famous coach newly arrived from college football. His name? Jock Sutherland. The Dodgers will rank 2nd in the Eastern Division.

JAMES D. CASTAGNOLI

C
Stanford
None

1949 co-captain of Stanford football team.

ART CASTELLI

G
NYU
1941 Churchill Pros (AA-Independent

Castelli plays in the team of Springfield, MA, which will substitute the Providence Steamrollers.

COSMO «FRANK» CASTIGLIA

T
Waynesburg
1949 Eire Vets-WilkesBarre Bullets (AFL-Independent)

During the same season he plays in at least 2 teams, working hard in the middle of the field.

JAMES V. «JIM» CASTIGLIA

FB-LB
Georgetown
1941 Philadelphia Eagles (NFL)
1942Philadelphia Eagles (NFL)
1945 Philadelphia Eagles (NFL)
1946 Philaldeplhia Eagles (NFL)
1947 Baltimore Colts (AAFC)-Washington Redskins (NFL)
1948 Washington Redskins (NFL)
Games: 40; Rushing: 313, yards 1,055, TDs 10; Rec.: 33, yards 236, TDs 2; Kick-Ret.:10, yards 244

After a good experience in the college football and one Orange Bowl (1st of January 1941), Castiglia is chosen by Pittsburgh and put under contract by Philadelphia. The first year as a pro is full of satisfactions: 11 games, 4 TDs scored. A pro contract also with the baseball team of Phila (American League), then the war: his sense of duty will drive Castiglia to wearing the uniform and taking part to WW II between 1943 and 1944.

After a 3 years break he will be back in 1945 for one single game with the Eagles: 13 runs, 29 yards. The ice is broken.

Castiglia will play again as a pro with the Eagles and then with the Redskins. He will arrive to Washington in 1947, After a quick passage (just one game) in the AAFC. With the Redskins he will dispute 2 great years, gaining an average of at least 400 yards per season.

Not so bad for a vet.

AL CEMENTINA

CB
San Jose State
None.

One of the best in the defensive line of the Spartans of San Jose St., author of 6 intercepts in the 1948 season.

SONNY CERTISSAMO

B
Santa Clara
1949 Jersey City Giants (AFL)

One of the more than 40 players who played in the farm club of the Giants in 1949.

CHARLES J. «CHUCK» CHERUNDOLO

C-LB
Penn State
1937 Cleveland Rams (NFL)
1938 Cleveland Rams (NFL)
1939 Cleveland Rams (NFL)
1940 Philadelphia Eagles (NFL)

1941 Pittsburgh Steelers (NFL)
1942 Pittsburgh Steelers (NFL)
1945 Pittsburgh Steelers (NFL)
1946 Pittsburgh Steelers (NFL)
1947 Pittsburgh Steelers (NFL)
1948 Pittsburgh Steelers (NFL)
Games: 106; Int. 5, yards 33

More than 100 games in 10 years of NFL career (including a «war break» in 1943–1944).

Chuck was for years one of the best centers of the league, also in the years from 1937 to 1941, when he was playing in low-chart teams, ranking last in their divisions. As the captain of the Steelers he will know his first winning season in 1942 (7–4–0).

During the off seasons he always worked as a successful business executive in Pittsburgh.

He was included among the Bowman cards dedicated to the pro football champions.

JOHN CHIMENTO

G
TCU
1946 Newark Bombers (AFL)
1948 Paterson Panthers (AFL)
1948 AFL Playoffs
1948 AFL Title

A guard in the farm team partecipated by the Chicago Bears, Chimento moves to Paterson (a team linked to Philaldelphia Eagles) in 1948, and there he gains a title of the league.

PETER «POUNDING PETE» CIGNETTI

FB-DB
Boston College
1940 Providence Steamrollers (AA)
1940 Cotton Bowl
Boston College Varsity Club Athletic Hall of Fame

Pete is one of the stars of the 1939 Boston College Eagles, the first team in the history of the college to qualify for a bowl; he is a tough and determined fullback who in 1990 will be elected to the Boston College Hall of Fame. His experience as a pro is not very incisive.

JOE CIPPICIANI

G-T
Scranton
1946 Bethlehem Bulldogs (AFL)

Cippiciano plays with a farm club adored by the audiences (the average for a single game is 10,000 attending people).

THOMAS A. «TOM» COLELLA

DB-RB-P
Canisius
1942 Detroit Lions (NFL)
1943 Detroit Lions (NFL)
1944 Cleveland Rams (NFL)
1945 Cleveland Rams (NFL)
1946 Cleveland Browns (AAFC)
1947 Cleveland Browns (AAFC)
1948 Cleveland Browns (AAFC)
1949 Buffalo Bills (AAFC)
Games : 37; Rushing: 137, yards 507, TDs 4; Rec.: 10, yards 127; TDs 3; FGs 1; Punting 56, yards 2,171; Kret.: 17, yards 394; Pret.: 9, yards 100; Int.4, Yds. 63(NFL stats).

Games: 52; Rushing 62, yards 246, TDs 4; Int. 21, yards 323, TD 1; Punting 141, yards 5,201, Avg 36,9
1945 Western Division Title
1945 NFL Champion
1946 AAFC West Division Title
1946 AAFC Champion
1947 AAFC West Division Title
1947 AAFC Champion
1948 AAFC West Division Title
1948 AAFC Champion

A difficult debut in a team bound to lose all the games of the season; as to Colella, he is apolyvalent athlete who runs, passes, receives and most importantly kicks and returns punts.

In 1943 the Lions are not the worst team in the league and so manage to get some satisfactions winning 3 games.

In 1944 Colella moves to Cleveland; with the Rams, still rebuilding their team under the lead of Buff Donelli, Tom will be the best runner of the team. The following year he goes on playing with consistency (10 games out of 10) and thanks to the superior skills of QB Waterfield, he will win the divisional title and will have the chance to play the NFL Championship Game on his home field against Washington. It is the 18th of December and it is a victory: 15–14.

In 1946 moves to the Browns, the team in which he will know 3 years of successes winning the title also in AAFC. In the 1946 finals he will register 4 receivings for a total 14 yards and 2 punts (average 38,5); in the finals of 1947 he will run for 6 yards, receive twice and complete 1 kick return; In 1948 he will bring home his third title in a row with 1 run, 2 punts, 1 punt return and 1 interception return. In 1949 he ends his career full of honour with the Buffalo Bills, realizing 3 intercepts in the course of the season.

VINCENT J. «VINCE» COMMISA

G—HC
Notre Dame
1944 Boston Yanks (NFL)

1946 Jersey City Giants (AFL)
1947 Jersey City Giants (AFL)
1948 Jersey City Giants (AFL) player—assistant coach
1949 Jersey City Giants (AFL)player—head coach
Games:1(NFL)
1943 College Football National Champion
1946 AFL All-League Team
1946 AFL Divisional Title
1946 AFL Title

In the years of the college he plays with the Fighting Irish together with Angelo Bertelli.

The NFL will be a quick experience for Commisa: only 1 game disputed. The passage is offered by the Yanks, the new Boston franchise organised by a music agent. In 1946 we find him in the farm club of the Giants: in the minor league he will find a good spotlight for 3 more seasons.

(A bit of trivia: in the AFL roster he figures as «Cammisa», while in the NFL registers he is archived as «Commisa», as everywhere else).

During his last year in Jersey City, after one season as an assistant coach under Ed Franco, he will be head coach and guard at the same time.

ANTHONY «TONY» COMPAGNO

FB-DB
St. Mary's (Cal)
1946 Pittsburgh Steelers (NFL)
1947 Pittsburgh Steelers (NFL)
1948 Pittsburgh Steelers (NFL)
Games: 34; Rushing: 125, yards 444, TDs 3; Rec.: 18, yards 295. TD 1; Fumbles 18; Int. 12

After playing with the football college team of St. Mary's coached by Len Casanova, Compagno lands to the NFL team of Art Rooney. Apart from being a fighting defensive back, he will become the second best runner of the Steelers, behind the formidable and talked-about Bill «Bullett» Dudley. For Tony and Co.

a second place in the divisional ranking of 1947. IN 1948 the sudden death of the coach throws the team in a season of unfrequent highs and very deep lows (4–8–0). For Compagno, 12 difficult games in a 12 games season. His last in the NFL, anyway.

The Bowman football card dedicated to him says: «*The Wild Bull of Pacific Coast ... considered one of the hardest line plungers in the NFL ...* "

ENIO E. CONTI   Born in italy

T
Bucknell
1938 New Jersey Giants (AA)
1940 Jersey City Giants(AA)
1941 Jersey City Giants (AA)-Philadelphia Eagles (NFL)
1942 Philadelphia Eagles (NFL)
1943 Phialdelphia Eagles-Pittsburgh Steelers (NFL)
1944 Philadelphia Eagles (NFL)
1945 Philadelphia Eagles (NFL)
1946 Bethlehem Bulldogs (AFL) head-coach
1938, 1940 AA Title
1942 NFL All-Stars Game

Enio is born in Napoli (Italy) on the 15th of February 1913. At the age of 25 he debuts in the American Association, also winning one championship. In 1941 the NFL opens his doors to him; Conti will remain among the pros for 6 long and tough years. In 1941 he is on the line covering rookie Tommy Thompson. The years 1942–1944 are marked by the war; Conti and the Eagles live their life in the low regions of the chart. In 1945 comes the first winning season after many years. But at the age of 32 it's time to quit. The following year Conti is the new head coach of the Eagles farm club playing in the AFL (5–4–1 the record).

GEORGE CONTI

B
Rhode Island Univ.
1941 Churchill Pros (AA-Independent)

1942 Springfield Steamrollers (AA)

In 1941 he is one of the many paisà playing in the Massachesetts team. that will end the season with a record of 6–5–0. The following year he plays again in the same city, in the team born merging Churchill Pros and Providence Steamrollers.

THOMAS J. «T.J.» TOM CORBO

G-LB
Duquesne
1944 Cleveland Rams (NFL)
Games: 10; Int. 1

A rocky guard in the early 40s when he played with the Dukes of the Duquesne University led by Buff Donelli, a team which in the glorious season of 1941 hit a record of 8–0–0 making it to the nation's Top 5. In 1944 he follows Donelli to Cleveland. Donelli is building the new Rams, fostering a competitive team out of rookies and free agents. Unfortunately the fruits of this work will be picked only by their successors: neither Donelli nor Corbo will be on the field the following year, when the Rams will reach the NFL finals.

JOE COTTONE

HB
Dartmouth
1941 Hartford Blues (Independent-AA)

He is in the roster of a team that in the course of the season will yield many of his players to the NY Yankees. After the war, he will find a role in an AFL team.

VICTOR CUCCIA

C
St.Mary's
None
1945 Sugar Bowl

A good center in a competitive college of the 40s.

EMILIO «MIMS» DADDARIO

HB-HC
Wesleyan
1940 Providence Steamrollers (AA)
1941 Hartford Blues (Independent-AA)
1942 Hartford Blues (AA)player-coach; Springfield Steamrollers (AA)
1940 AA All-League Team

He is the 3rd best runner in the 1940 season of the American Association.

In 1942 he moves to the Blues (where he will score 7 points). The gazettes will talk of him also for romantic business: shortly before the beginning of a game he leaves the field for a date with his future wife. For a short period he will play and coach the team of Lou Viscusi.

LOUIS W. «BILL» DADDIO

DE-OE
Pittsburgh
1941 Chicago Cardinals (NFL)
1942 Chicago Cardinals (NFL)
1946 Buffalo Bisons (AAFC)
Games: 22; Rec. 5, yards 39 ; Rushing : 11, yards 8 ; TD 1 ;PAT 16–17 ; FGs 9–18 ; Points 49
In AAFC: Games 3; PATs 3–3; Points 3
1938 All-American

He arrives to NFL after a good college career; he debuts with the Cardinals of Conzelman in a season of few lights and many shadows (3–7–1). Daddio is displayed in defense and offense, and he also kicks PATs and FGs. Also for him and the Cards a 1942 season marked by the rumours of war. Daddio will take part to the military operations between 1943 and 1945, saying goodbye to the NFL.

Said farewell to the arms, Daddio will be back on the playing fields in 1946, playing some games with the Bisons in the new AAFC league and scoring all his PATs. But by this time he is over 30, and the desire to play at certain levels is gone. Life goes on.

Also for him a place on a Topps card.

ROBERT «BOB» DAL PORTO

HB
Cal
None

He takes part to the *Big Game* of 1947.

FRANCIS A. «FRANK» DAMIANI

T
Manhattan
1944 New York Giants (NFL)
Games: 4
1944 Eastern Division Title
1944 NFL Championship Game

He debuts in the NFL with a winning team, even if a bit «blocked» by the strong Frank Cope. For him only a quick apparition in the finals lost to the Packers. Then, the war.

GEORGE DE FERRARI

T
?
1942 Paterson Panthers (AA)

DeFerrari is in the roster of the team coached by Dale Burnett.

EUGENE DE FILIPPIS

HB
Santa Clara
None
1949 Orange Bowl

A regular of the Broncos in 1949 (8–2–1): a competitive and hard team.

LOUIS P. «LOU» DE FILIPPO

C-G-LB
Fordham
1941 New York Giants (NFL)
1945 New York Giants (NFL)
1946 New York Giants (NFL)
1947 New York Giants (NFL)
Games: 47
1940 Fordham Captain
1940 All-Team Cotton Bowl
1941 NFL Eastern Division Title
1941 NFL Championship Game
1945 NFL Eastern Division Title
1945 NFL Championship Game
Fordham University Hall of Fame

DeFilippo gets in the spotlight in the forgery of Fordham; in the years 1938–1940 he is a regular center, leader of the offense together with QBs William Krywicki and Angelo Fortunato and FBs Dom Principe and Stephen Filipowicz. In his first NFL year, he disputes all the 11 games of the regular season alongside the great Mel Hein, winning the divisional title and disputing a Championship Game ruined by the attack to Pearl Harbor (the Chicago Bears will win 37–9). After that, three years in the war.

DeFilippo will be back on the fields in 1945: a winning season, with a large audience (the Giants registrer an average of 50,000 attending people in the home games) and a big disappointment at the 15th December Championship: a defeat that is a perfect copy of the one of 1941 against the Chicago Bears (this time the final score is 24–14).

The Giants fall directly from the stars to the stable and in 1947 they arrive last in the division registering 8 defeas over 12 games; the 31 years old DeFilippo is arrived to his final stop and plays only 4 times.

ALFRED DE LUCIA

T
Duquesne
None

A regular of the team unbeaten in 1941 (8–0–0).

MARIO DE MARCO

G-LB
Miami (Fl)
1949 Detroit Lions (NFL)
Games : 12

At the college he plays with the Hurricans a good 1946 season (record 8–2–0). Two years later DeMarco disputes one full NFL season with the Lions, which are slowly building a valid team. A mighty player, with some physical trouble.

SPIRO DELL'ERBA

LB-FB
Ohio State
1947 Cleveland Browns (AAFC)
1948 Baltimore Colts (AAFC)
1949 Baltimore Colts (AAFC)—Erie Vets (AFL-Independent)
Games : 31; Rush.: 31, yards 176; Rec.: 1, yards 14; KRt.: 2, yards 42; Int.: 2, yards 18 (AAFC)
1945 Big10 Championship

1947 AAFC West Division Title
1947 AAFC Champion

A very good experience in college with the Ohio State Buckeyes, culminating with the 1945 title.

Dell'Erba becomes a pro with the best of AAFC: the Cleveland Browns project. He is a rookie who will play 8 games, displayed both in defence and in offense, winning a divisional title and an AAFC title.

In 1948 he moves to the Colts: the QB is «a certain» Y.A. Tittle, 21 years old and great numbers to show.

Dell'Erba will remain in Baltimore for 2 seasons, playing in the last as a linebacker. He will also register a short passage in the AFL.

FRANK DELMONICO

E
Holy Cross
1941 Providence Steamrollers (AA)—Churchill Pros

A difficult debut in a team that will abandon the championship after only 3 games. Some of the players will move to the AFL teams and some others (among whom Delmonico) they will join the Churchill Pros of Springfield, MA, trying to end the season.

MIKE DE NOIA

E
Scranton
None.
1945, 1948 Little All-American
1948 All-State
The University of Scranton Wall of Fame

An athlete capable of winning both on a football field (he will be a starter for 4 years) and on a basketball ground (he will be top scorer nel in 1948).

CARMINE R. «RIP» DE PASCAL

DE-OE
Wichita State
1945 Pittsburgh Steelers(NFL)
Games: 1

A discrete college player whose impact on NFL is not one of the best. The only positive note is that he is on the field in the occasione of the two only seasonal victories of the team.

CARL DE SALVO

C
St. Mary's
None
1945 Sugar Bowl

He is a regular in the 1945 team, ranking 7th nationwide (7–2–0).

ALBERT J. «DE RO» DE ROGATIS

C-T
Duke
1949 New York Giants (NFL)
1950 New York Giants (NFL)
1951 New York Giants (NFL)
1952 New York Giants (NFL)
Games: 43; 12 Points
1944 All-State
1948 Duke Team Captain
1948 All American
1951 NFL All-Pro

A player in the spotlight since high school: in the Central High years he is one of the best athletes of the state. He will then move to the Duke University (1945–

1948), where he will be voted All-American tackle at the end of the 1948 season. Chosen at the 2nd round by the Giants, DeRogatis will debut in the NFL with the growing team led by coach Steve Owen. During the season he will take advantage of a fumble to realize his first exceptional points. 1950, the year of the «umbrella defense», will bring DeRogatis and his teammates the 2nd rank in the conference; the Giants will end their season with a good 10–2–0. In 1951 the Giants will again rank 2nd after the great Cleveland Browns and the always stronger «De Ro» will be selected as an All-Pro, together with 3 teammates of his. The New York team is solid. The same rank will be reached again once in his last season with the Giants. An ankle injury ends his career. After the retiremente he will work from 1953 for an insurance company and will commentate football games for the WNEW radio station; in 1960 he will move to the NBC TV and from 1966 he will be one of the main anchors of a sports programme.

DANIEL J. «DAN» DE SANTIS

HB-DB
Niagara
1941 Philadelphia Eagles (NFL)
Games: 11; Rushing: 45, yards 125; Passing: 3–7, yards 78, TD 1; Rec.: 4, yards 53; PRt.: 9. yards 80; KRt: 7, yards 205; PAT 1–1; Points 1

Here is a versatile athlete (in his rookie year he fills the books with great stats in only 11 games), rich of promises, who will give his best not on the playing field but in the theaters of war. NFL was a nice game, something to tell on the front and maybe to the grandsons.

DAVID E. «DAVE» DIFILIPPO

G
Villanova
1941 Philadelphia Eagles (NFL)
Games:5

He lands to NFL and disputes half of the season games. Great expectations, important teammates and then the war: 4 years serving the country on quite crueller fields.

AL DI MARCO

QB
Iowa
None
1943 Iowa MVP

He is a protagonist with the Hawkeyes, 1,105 yards and 6 TDs in one season, 1,794 yards and 17 TDs in the whole career.

RAIMONDO «RAY» DINI

QB-LB
None
1946 Bethlehem Bulldogs (AFL)
1947 Bethlehem Bulldogs (AFL)
1948 Bethlehem Bulldogs (AFL)
1949 Bethlehem Bulldogs (AFL)
1947 AFL Western Division Title
1947 AFL Title
1948 AFL All-League Team

A very young QB (only 19 years old) in the farm club kept under observation by the Philadelphia Eagles. In 1947 comes a divisional title and the title of the league; Dini realises 2 fundamental intercepts during the Championship Game against Paterson.

In 1949 he will be once again the king of intercepts in the AFL, reaching 8.

JOHN DI NUNZIO

C
New Britain Teachers
1942 Hartford Blues

He plays in the team together with player-coach Emilio «Mims» Daddario.

DAN DI RENZO

E
Southern
1948 Paterson Panthers (AFL)
1949 Paterson Panthers (AFL)
1950 Paterson Panthers (AFL)
Games:?; Tot. Points 66; TDs 10
1948 AFL Playoffs
1948 AFL Title
1949 AFL Playoffs
1949 AFL Championship Game
1948 AFL All-League Team

A good receiver who imposes himself in the AFL. He is one of the top scorers of the league and disputes 2 finals, bringing home one victory in 1948 an one defeat in 1949 (although he will complete 1 TD in the game). In 1950 he is still one of the best with 36 points (4th of the league) and 5 receiving TDs (2nd in the AFL).

NICK DI VIETRO

T
None
1949 Bethlehem Bulldogs (AFL)
1950 Bethlehem Bulldogs (AFL)
1949 AFL Playoffs

2 seasons in the AF beating a huge competition.

«RIPPER» DONATI

T
?
1946 Bethlehem Bulldogs (AFL)

A true truck, a formidable and fighting tackle.

ALDO T. «BUFF» DONELLI

C-HB-HC
Duquesne
1941 Pittsbugh Steelers (NFL) head-coach
1944 Cleveland Rams (NFL) head-coach
Games: 4–11–0 (coach)
1928–29 Soccer U.S. Amateur Cup

Born in 1907, Donelli is a good soccer player in the Morgan Strasser F.C. already at 22, when he gains the the nickname « Buff» because of his passion for Buffalo Bill Cody and his circus.

Between 1926 and 1929 he is a reliable center and an incisive runner at the Duquesne University; in 1929 he is also the captain of the football team that for the first time in the history of the college completes the season undefeated (9–0–1).

In the meanwhile he goes on playing soccer and is the best scorer in the Pittsburgh area; in 1928 he is hired by the Heidelberg F.C. and wins the Soccer U.S. Amateur Cup beating the Newark F.G. by 9–0 in the finals. «Buff» scores 5 goals.

Between 1930 and 1933, Donelli plays soccer with the Curry Silver Tops F.C. and in 1934 he is chosen to play with the USA national team in the World Cup held in Italy.

In the land of his parents Buff plays 2 official games, the first against Mexico (4 goals for him) and the second against Italy, scoring the only goal in a heavy defeat by 7–1 (Italy, though, will be the winning team in the World Cup).

At the end of the tournamente the Italian pro team of Lazio (playing in Rome) will offer Aldo a good contract, but he will prefer going back home.

The call of the gridiron is strong and so Aldo in 1939 is already a head-coach in his college; 10 years after his team captain season he will lead Duquesne to its second unbeaten season ever (8–0–1), ranking 10th nationwide. After a one-loss season in 1940, in 1941 comes a third undefeated season, the best and last in the college record-book.

Art Rooney, the co-owner of the Steelers, after two defeats at the beginning of the season calls Donelli to the deathbed of his team: he allows Aldo not to leave Duquesne, so Buff will train the Steelers in the morning and the Dukes in the afternoon. 5 games and 5 defeats later the NFL commissioner imposes Donelli a choice. Donelli says Duquesne.

In 1943 he is back playing soccer for the Morgan Strasser: in 2 years he will dispute 2 U.S. Open Cup finals.

Also in 1944 he comes back in the pro league as the leader of the Cleveland Rams while he serves with the U.S. Navy; once the NFL campaign ends, Donelli joins the military service.

But when the peace comes, Donelli starts his definitive college coaching career, at Boston University from 1947 to 1956 and at Columbia University from 1957 to 1967.

A bit of trivia:

- His son Richard, a professional dentist, in 1958 was the Lions MVP at Columbia as a quarterback.

- Boston University from 1995 assigns a yearly award, the *Aldo «Buff» Donelli Leadership Award Recipient*, to remember their 10 years football coach and 5 years Director of Athletics.

ALLEN A. «AL» DONELLI

HB
Duquesne
1941 Pittsburgh Steelers (NFL)
1942 Pittsburgh Steelers(NFL)
Games: 11; Pass:: 2–8, TD 1; Rush.17, yards 16; Rec.: 2, yards 25; PRt.: 1, yards 11; KRt.: 4, yards 4, yards 83; Int. 1, yards 18; Punt 1, yards 43

After having been in 1939 and 1940 the starter halfback of the winning Dukes (8–0–1 and 10th in the national ranking, 7–1–0 in the two tears—on the sideline the coach is the other Donelli, Aldo), Allen Donelli arrives to Pittsburgh in 1941. He will play for 2 years in the NFL before he is called to duty by the Army.

JOSEPH «JOE» D'ORAZIO

T
Ithaca
1944 Detroit Lions (NFL)
Games : 5

Giuseppe-Joseph passes through NFL for one single season; he is already 29 and knows the honour to play with Frankie Sinkwich in a nice winning season (6–3–1 the Lions record).

CARLO «CARL» FAGIOLO

G
None
1944 Philaldelphia Eagles (NFL)
Games: 2

Another one of the Italian-American Eagles; in 1944 the roster of Phila is a true Little Italy: Manzini, Canale, Banducci, Conti, Mandarino, Cabrelli, Ferrante. The team ends 2nd in the Eastern Division (7–1–2).

CARMEN (CARMINE) FALCONE

QB
Pennsylvania
1949 Paterson Panthers (AFL)
1950 Paterson Panthers (AFL)
1949 AFL Playoffs
1949 AFL Championship Game
1949 AFL All-League Team

In 1949 he is the second best QB of the league (60–132, yards 969, 11TDs pass) and leads the team through the playoffs and into the unlucky AFL finals (1 TD pass against Bethlehem and 2 TDs pass against the Richmond Rebels in the

Championship Game). In 1950 he will leave more positive marks in the seasonal stats of AFL.

GARY J. FAMIGLIETTI

FB-LB-HB
Boston University
1938 Chicago Bears (NFL)
1939 Chicago Bears (NFL)
1940 Chicago Bears (NFL)
1941 Chicago Bears (NFL)
1942 Chicago Bears (NFL)
1943 Chicago Bears (NFL)
1944 Chicago Bears (NFL)
1945 Chicago Bears (NFL)
1946 Boston Yanks (NFL)
Games: 88; Rushing: 528, yards 1,981, TDs 24; Rec. 12, yards 187, TD 1; Total Points 151.
1940 NFL Eastern Division Title
1940 NFL Champion
1940 All-Stars Game
1941 NFL Eastern Division Title
1941 NFL Champion
1942 NFL Eastern Division
1942 NFL Rushing TDs Top Scorer
1942 NFL Championship Game
1943NFL Eastern Division Title
1943 NFL Champion

After the great years with the Boston University Terriers (his performances against the rival Boston College are history) he will play in NFL tournaments for 9 years, at pretty respectable levels.

He begins in 1938 with a team which is strongly changing the roster; for Gary 9 games and some good action.

In 1939 arrives rookie star Sid Luckman and the Bears rank second in the Eastern, behind the Packers; Famiglietti disputes 10 games.

In 1940 comes the Division title and Famiglietti reveals himself as one of the most productive runners together with Nolting and Maniaci, realizing 4 TDs. The winning post-season sees the affirmation of the Bears in the NFL Championship Game in Washington: the Redskins are defeated by a tremendous 73–0!

Famiglietti scores a TD in the fourth quarter; his final record is 4 runs for 18 yards, and ends in the NFL Championship record-book.

In 1941 the Bears repeat themselves gaining the conference title with a record of 10–1–0; Gary plays only 7 games because of minor injuries and leaves no mark in the Championship won against the NY Giants (Chicago, 21st December: Bears-Giants 37–9).

1942 is an extraordinaire year for Famiglietti and the Bears: Gary disputes 10 regular season games, running 118 times for 503 yards (he is the team's top runner and the third in the league, but also the second best scorer of the NFL, behind the formidable Don Hutson of the Packers); the Bears end the regular season undefeated (11–0–0) and reach once again the finals. But in the 1942 Championship in Washington, Chicago unexpectedly loses 14–6 against the Redskins. To no avail Famiglietti carries the ball 7 times for a total 22 yards.

The season 1943 is the «usual» season: Division title (8–1–1) and NFL title (Bears-Redskins 41–21), with Famiglietti playing 10 games and scoring 2 TDs.

1944 is marked by the military obligations of 39 players of the team, among which the QB Sid Luckman, who serves in the Navy during the week and plays with the Bears in the week-end.

In 1945 the Bears know their first losing season since 1929, but 30 years old Famiglietti is still there running and carrying forth the ball: 10 games, 65 rush, 235 yards and 3 TDs against the adversaries.

Before quitting, in 1946 Gary gets back home to play his last NFL season among the Boston Yanks; football is nearing a new era, and even though the Yanks will rank last, Famiglietti scores 4 TDs in 11 games: the second best scorer in the team, behind a 22 years old receiver.

GASPER FARINA

B
Whitewater
1940 Kenosha Cardinals (AFL)

He plays as an unofficial AFL team member for one season: 15 games, 10 victories.

CLEMENTE «CLEM» FASCITELLI

G
Springfield
1941 Churchill Pros (AA-Independent)

From the campus to Pynchon Park, always in the same city. A short experience as a pro.

(A little trivia: in the same team played also Vince Lombardi, before his affirmation as a coach).

JACK FERRANTE

E-ED
none
1939 Wilmington Clippers (AA)
1940 Wilmington Clippers (AA)
1941 Wilmington Clippers (AA)
1941 Philadelphia Eagles (NFL)
1944 Philadelphia Eagles (NFL)
1945 Philadelphia Eagles (NFL)
1946 Philadelphia Eagles (NFL)
1947 Philadelphia Eagles (NFL)
1948 Philadelphia Eagles (NFL)
1949 Philadelphia Eagles (NFL)
1950 Philadelphia Eagles (NFL)

*Games: 81; Receiving: 169, yards 2,894, TDs 31; KRt.: 7, yards 99; Total Points
186 (NFL stats only)*
1939 AA Leading Scorer
1939 AA All-League Team
1941 AA All-League Team
1941 AA Title (2 TDs in Championship Game)
1947 NFL Eastern Division Title
1947 NFL Championship Game
1948 NFL Eastern Division Title
1948 NFL Champion
1949 NFL Eastern Division Title
1949 NFL Champion
2 High School City Championship
Eagles Great of the Past
1940s ALL-DECADE TEAM (chosen by the Pro Football Hall of Fame Selection Committee menbers)

Jack's family comes from New Jersey; his parents, born in Italy, have to move for work and settle down in Philadelphia in 1926. There Jack attends high school for a while, but quits before time to work in a convenience store. In 1933 he discovers football and starts playing for an amateurial team. Local sportsmen and journalists appreciate his qualities and in one year's time he is called to play for the team of Seymour in a semipro league of Pennsylvania; he will begin with a hire of 7 dollars per game that will soon grow to 25.

Ferrante is put under contract by the Eagles in 1939, and initially is destined to the satellite team of Wilmington, playing in the American Association. Here's a *paisà* with no college experience but a great talent for reading the trajectories on the field.

1939 is for him a major season in the minor league: best scorer with 54 points, best receiver with 8 TDs.

He will remain with the Clippers until 1943; there will be an interlude in 1941 when the Eagles provide his debut in the NFL: 3 games and 2 receivings later they send him back to Wilmington.

In 1944 comes the second call from Philadelphia and Jack is fast to get it; he and Van Buren are the rookies that give the Eagles what was needed, bringing a seasonal record of 7–1–2 and the second ranking in the division.

1945 brings another second place in the Eastern and the affirmation of Ferrante, who is the best receiver of the team (Rec. 21; yards 464, Tds 7) and ranks 7th in the NFL.

The following year coach «Grease» Neale decides to use Ferrante only in offense (between 1941 and 1945 he had played both in offense and defense); also this new season sees a winning record and the second place in the division.

In 1947 finally comes the victory in the Eastern and a passport for the NFL Championship Game; the final result, though, will pay the Chicago Cardinals (28–21), with the Eagles hard to die and fighting until the last quarter.

1948 represents the revenge of the Eagles: after arriving first in the Eastern, they face again the Cardinals for the NFL title, and the 19th December, in the snow, at the first action QB Tommy Thompson unexpectedly throws a long bomb (65 yards) to Jack Ferrante in end zone: TD canceled for an offside penalty! The game restarts in a power running contest; it will end with a 7–0 victory for the Eagles. 36,000 fans had bought the ticket for the game, but only 28,000 have made it to the stadium sieged by the snow.

The 1949 season brings another division title and an NFL Championship Game; this time the adversaries are the Los Angeles Rams, confronted in the Coliseum under a storm. The same year Jack gets in the Bowman cards collection. The Eagles will win 14–0.

1950 is Ferrante's last year in the NFL, played with the usual accuracy and the acknowledged quality: 12 games, 588 yards and 3 TDs (he is the team best receiver and the 11th in the league). The NFL has changed, the AAFC teams have arrived and new conferences have been created. Jack will not accept to move to Detroit and will retire from pro football, deciding to work as a salesman for the Ortlieb Brewing. In 1953 he will start a parallel career as a high school coach, a career that will continue among many satisfactions until 1961. The final retirement will arrive in 1977, with a load of good memories an some important acknowledgements.

PETE FERRANTINO

C
Hofstra
1942 Long Island Clippers (AA)

He plays 1 season with the Clippers, often pointed out as the «Ken Strong's All-Stars» in honour to the strong 36 years old player of the team.

JOHN «BIG JOHN» FERRARO

T
USC
None.
1943 Pacific Coast Conference Champ
1943 Rose Bowl
1944 All-American
1944 Pacific Coast Conference Champ
1944 Rose Bowl
1947 All-Coast Team
1947 All-American 2 nd team
1947 Rose Bowl
1973 NCAA Silver Anniversary Award
COLLEGE FOOTBALL HALL OF FAME

«Superman» or «Hercules», as the enthustic journalists of the *Los Angeles Times* called this tackle, was a protagonist in the all-time history of the Southern California Trojans, marking with his formidable presence on field the most extraordinaire years of the team (between 1943 and 1947, 2 PCC titles and 3 Rose Bowls). In 1943, during his freshman season, Ferraro will be chosen as All-American and his team will conquer the conference and beat Washington by 29–0 in the Rose Bowl.

As a sophomore, in 1944 he will repeat the performance winning the conference title and taking part to the second consecutive victory in the Rose Bowl against Tennessee: 25–0 the final score, and for him another All-American title.

In 1945 he will serve in the Navy.

Back to the USC in 1946, after a pause for an injury he will win yet another conference title with the Trojans and will bring home his third Rose Bowl. At the end of college Ferraro will join the LAPD, and his shirt with the number 71 will end framed on a wall in his house.

ROBERT «BOB» FERRI

FB
Syracuse
1949 Jersey City Giants (AFL)
1949 AFL All-League Team

Among the 10 top runners of the AFL in 1949, the weakness of the team notwithstanding (record: 1–9–0 and last ranking of the season).

ALBERT M. «AL» FIORENTINO

G-LB
Boston College
1943 Washington Redskins (NFL)
1944 Washington Redskins (NFL)
1945 Boston Yanks (NFL)
Games: 28; Int. 1; KRt. 1, Yds. 5
1942 Orange Bowl
1943 NFL Eastern Division Title
1943NFL Championship Game

Fiorentino turns out to be a great guard in Boston College, disputing the 1942 Orange Bowl. In his first year as a pro he wins the Division with Dutch Bergman's Redskins, and on the 26th of December 1943 he is on field to dispute the NFL Championship Game in Chicago. Not so bad for a rookie (even if the final score will be 41–21 for the Bears).

In 1944 the new offensive system introduced by coach DeGroot (the T-formation) needs a period of adaptation from the Skins, which will find their balance only in the second half of the season. They will rank third with a 6–3–1; Fiorentino will play all the games and will be the protagonist of a decisive intercept.

In 1945 Fiorentino is sold to Boston; his coming home is not something to remember: playing with a team with no character floating in the low regions of the ranking, he will dispute his last 8 NFL games.

EDWARD A. «ED» FIORENTINO

DE
Brown
1947 Boston Yanks (NFL)
Games: 4

Coming from the League, where he was one of the 1943 Brown University leading players, Fiorentino is picked by Boston at the 10th round of the 1944 draft, but the military service will keep him off the fields until 1947, when his debut takes place in a team which thanks to new coach Clipper Smith starts gaining some prestigious victories in the course of the regular season. Fiorentino will dispute only 4 games.

ALDO J. FORTE

G-T
Montana
1939 Chicaco Bears (NFL)
1940 Chicago Bears (NFL)
1941 Chicago Bears (NFL)
1946 Detroit Lions-Chicago Bears (NFL)
1947 Green Bay Packers (NFL)
Games: 49
1940 NFL Western Division Title
1940 NFL Champion
1941 NFL Western Division Title
1941 NFL Champion
1946 NFL Western Division Title
1946 NFL Champion

Already in the regular team in his first NFL year, Aldo witnesses the Bears' second ranking in the Western Division in 1939. In 1940 it gets even better: the Bears conquer the division and dispute the NFL Championship Game with a smashing victory over the Redskins. Same story the following year, when a good season of the team (led in all the gams by Forte himself) will bring another NFL title.

When the echo of the victory dissipates, Aldo confronts 4 long years of war, after which he is back to try again a career with the oval ball. He signs with Detroit, plays 3 games and then moves to his second house address: the Bears. It is a big style return, and he deserves the Division title and the NFL finals. An audience of 60,000 gather in the Giants stadium to *really* enjoy the big game; the final score will be 24–14 for Chicago, decisively reinforced by the return of its many vets.

Aldo Forte is already 29 when he decides he will not be put aside and allows himself one last NFL year signing with the Green Bay Packers of Curly Lambeau. The team will begin the new season adopting the T-formation and the «old» guard will have some more good time.

ROBERT D. «CHICK» FORTE

HB-DB-LB
Arkansas
1946 Green Bay Packers (NFL)
1947 Green Bay Packers (NFL)
1948 Green Bay Packers (NFL)
1949 Green Bay Packers (NFL)
1950 Green Bay Packers (NFL)
1952 Green Bay Packers (NFL)
1953 Green Bay Packers (NFL)
Games: 80; Rushing: 107, yards 331, Fumble 4; Rec. 24, yards 242, TDs 3; INT. 23, yards 291; KRt. 14; yards 290; PR. 2, yards 28; Passing: 8–14; yards 64, TD 1

Chosen in the 9th round, Chick arrives to Green Bay the year a star retires: Don Hutson. At the doors of the windy city of the Packers a long period of low luck (only the arrival of Vince Lombardi in far away 1959 will bring the green-yellow team back to its glory days), yet Forte will make his share, he will enjoy himself covering different roles, forcing some fumbles and realising 23 intercepts. In the years 1946–1947 the team will also hit winning records (6–5–0 and 6–5–1), while there will be real troubles in 1948,when the players will be heavily fined because of their low yield. But as the wise men say, *«Once you reach the bottom, you can still start digging»*. 1949 will be a nightmare for Forte and his teammates: they will suffer the worst record ever in the history of the Packers. In 1950 the team continues to lose, even after the restructuration of the league, which merges with the AAFC and creates two new conferences (the Packers will be included in the National together with other 7 teams). Forte is called on duty by the Army, forced to enroll also the reservists because of the crisis in Korea.

In 1952, the 30 years old veteran from Arkansas will be back on the fields, for a season in which he will play all the games contributing to the improvement of the Packers record (6–6–0).

1953 is his last season in the league: 11 games and a new role as a linebacker.

BILL «BUTCH» FORTUNATO

B
Fordham
1940 Newark Bears (AA)

One season in a farm club owned by a team from NFL.

STEVE FORTUNATO

G
Alabama
1949 Erie Vets (AFL-Independent)

A short experience far from home.

ALFRED «AL» FRANCESCONI

E
J. Carroll
None
1942 All-Big Four in basketball
John Carroll Athletic Hall of Fame

1941–42 leading player and top scorer in football and basketball at J.Carroll. Once retired he settles in Akron, OH, where he serves as a volunteer and enjoys his time playing golf.

DOMINIC «MICKEY» FRINZI

HB
Villanova
None

Starter in the 1949 team of Villanova (a winning season: 8–1–0), Frinzi collects sound victories against Boston College, Texas A&M, Penn State, Duquesne, North Carolina State.

ANTHONY «TONY» FUSALARO

T
Northeastern
1946 Long Island Indians (AFL)
1948 Wilmington Clippers (AFL)
1948 AFL Playoffs
1948 AFL Championship Game

In 1946 he plays in the farm team of the Boston Yanks, ending the season with a record of 5–5–0 and the 2nd ranking in the Eastern Division of AFL.

Two years later we find him in the AFL playing for the Clippers; he will make it to the playoffs and to the finals of the league (defeated by the Paterson Panthers).

DOM FUSCI

T
South Carolina
1948 Paterson Panthers (AFL)
1948 AFL Playoffs
1948 AFL Title

One of the paisà registered in the roster of the 1948 AFL champions.

JOE FUSELLA

G
Miami
1949 Jersey City Giants (AFL)

Also for him a quick passage in AFL.

LUCIANO «GALLOPING LOU» «LU» GAMBINO

FB-LB
Indiana-Maryland
1948 Baltimore Colts (AAFC)
1949 Baltimore Colts (AAFC)
Games: 19; Rush.: 102, yards 402, TDs 2; Rec.: 16, yards 95, TD 1; KRt.: 3, yards 57

In 1947 he is one of the biggest players for the Terrapins of Maryland and, with 16 TDs and 96 points, the nation's scoring leader.

In 1948 he arrives to the NFL, strongly awaited by the fans of the Colts. He will be one of the 4 used by coach Cecil Isbell, but he will not be the best of all. Baltimore will end the season 2nd.

The following year the team is in deep crisis. Isbell will pay the price for this, substituted with Driskill; but better results will not come. The only good news will be the passes of QB Y.A. Tittle and the good season of Lou Gambino, who will complete 56 carryings for a total 208 yards. Not a great record, but the other runners in the team did even worse …

FELIX «ATLAS» GANGEMI

C
Fordham
1941 Jersey City Giants (AA)
1941 AA Playoffs
1941 AA All-League Team

He is one of most acclaimed players in the Roosevelt Stadium, where the Giants play their home games. The season will end witha 4–4–0 and small-measure defeat in the playoffs (7–6).

WILLIAM «BILL» GARGIULO (GARGUILO)

B
None
1949 Jersey City Giants (AFL)

Gargiulo is a very common surname in Italy; in the archives of the AFL it appears with some letters postponed. William-Guglielmo is one of the many who have a try with the Giants. A short story.

MICHAEL J. «MIKE» GARZONI

G
Fresno State, USC
1947 Washington Redskins (NFL)
1948 New York Giants (NFL)—New York New York Yankees (AAFC)
Games: 15 (NFL); 2(AAFC)

After a college career under the spotlights, Grazoni is chosen at the 6th round of the 1947 draft by the Washington Redskins.

In the same year he debutsin the team of the capital city, led in offense by Sammy Baugh.

In 1948 he moves to New York, where he will play 5 games with the Giants and 2 with the AAFC Yankees.

ANGELO R. «BOB» GAUDIO

OG-LB-DG
Ohio State
1947 Cleveland Browns (AAFC)
1948 Cleveland Browns (AAFC)
1949 Cleveland Browns (AAFC)
1951 Cleveland Browns (NFL)
Games: 39 (AAFC); 12, KRt.: 1, yards 8 (NFL)
1947 AAFC West division Title
1947 AAFC Champion
1948 AAFC West division Title
1948 AAFC Champion
1949 AAFC West division Title
1949 AAFC Champion
1951 NFL American Conference Title
1951 NFL Championship Game

A highly respectable guard in college, Bob Gaudio is put under contract by the Browns, the team which will smash the AAFC; there will be years of great success for Bob and his teamamtes, 3 times champions of the league. After a one year break he will be back in 1951, to play the NFL championship; here also the Browns will be among the best (7 finals between 1950 and 1957, with 3 titles).

FRANK J. GAZIANO   **Born in Italy**

G
Holy Cross
1942 Worcester Panthers (AA)
1944 Boston Yanks (NFL)
Games: 9

Francesco (Frank) Giuseppe (Joseph) Gaziano is born on the 5th of February 1916 in Montereale (Italy). After the college and a short apprenticeship in the pro minor league American Association (where he realizes 1 TD in the 1942 season), he debuts in the NFL with the new Boston team set up by singers manager

Ted Collins with the money gained selling the war bonds of his artists. The roster is packed with wilful debutants, pefected by vets cut out from other teams and led by George Cafego, a good and not much used QB who had been first choice in 1940.

The seasonal record will not be that good (2–8–0), but it will count a much felt victory on the Brooklyn Tigers. For Gaziano it will remain his only pro year, something to tell his grandsons.

His integration in the New World (immigration, learning of a new language, high school, college and the tipically American sport) was anyway very fast, surely easened by the wealth of his family.

ARTHUR L. GEROMETTA

OT-DT
Illinois-Army
None.
1945 All-American Look Magazine
Indiana Hall of Fame

A very good athlete in high school, City and State Championship with Emerson High. After one year at the Illinois University he receives a call from Red Blaik and moves to Army. They will be years of successes, national titles, press articles.

MARIO «YO-YO» GIANNELLI

DG-OG
Boston College
1948 Philadelphia Eagles (NFL)
1949 Philadelphia Eagles (NFL)
1950 Philadelphia Eagles (NFL)
1951 Philadelphia Eagles (NFL)
Games: 49
1942 OrangeBowl
1948 College All-Star Game
1948 NFL Eastern Division Title

1948 NFL Champion
1949 NFL Eastern Division Title
1949 NFL Champion
Boston College Varsity Club Athletic Hall of Fame

Giannelli reveals himself at Boston College: a defensive and offensive guard of great quality.

In 1948, after the College All-Stars, he is in the NFL with the Eagles. He is an extra-sized lineman, tough and quick, a tragedy for his adversaries; the Eagles of Thompson and Van Buren reach the top of the division and win the NFL title NFL and Yo-Yo Giannelli is there with them.

Then in 1949 happens the same: divisional title and NFL crown (this time against the Los Angeles Rams, final score of 14–0). The new decade will bring many troubles to the team of Philadelphia: economic problems, injuries and a deluding championship. 1951 opens with a new coach and a new QB; Neale gets fired e Thompson retires. Giannelli is already 30 years old and weighs 260 lbs. (the heaviest of his team). But out there on the field the things become more and more difficult: new teams, new schemes, new champions. The Bears slide to the last ranking of their division (4–8–0) and Mario is out of the league. He had been an oustanding guard and a two times World Champion.

JOE GIANOTTI

G
Boston University
1940 Paterson Panthers (AA)
1941 Paterson Panthers (AA)
1942 Paterson Panthers (AA)
1940 AA Playoffs
1941 AA Playoffs

A guard displayed by the Panthers (with an agreement with New York Giants) for 2 seasons; Gianotti will contribute to the conquer of the playoffs.

JOE GIANTONIO

G
Fordham
1946 Paterson Panthers (AFL)

On of the Hinchcliffe Stadium fighters.

ROBERT «BOB» GHILOTTI

DB
Stanford
None

During a game in 1948 Ghilotti intercepts and returns straight to TD a ball played by the adversaries.

PIETRO ORIS «PETE» GORGONE   **Born in Italy**

LB-HB
Muhlenberg
1946 New York Giants (NFL)
1948 Bethlehem Bulldogs (AFL)
Games: 9 (NFL)
1946 NFL Eastern Division Title
1946 NFL Championship Game

Born in Bruca, a little town in Sicily (Italy), Gorgone arrives to the States very young and immediately grasps the occasions offered by the Big Country: instruction, sports and work.

He has the luck of debuting in the NFL with a team acclaimed by the fans (50,000 in average) that makes points over points and arrives to the top of the Eastern Division. In the December of 1946 the Giants are on field for the finals in front of 58,000 fans, against the favourite Bears. Unfortunately during the morning the news explode: 2 Giants players are investigated for a story of bribings. The Bears will win the title by 24–14, although the Giants end their game gaining points. To Gorgone the NFL was a very short experience. We will find him in 1948, aged 27, playing in the AFL with the team of Bethlehem, league champion in 1947.

It will be a complicated season because of the new rules: the salary cap was reduced from $ 6,000 to $ 2,000 per game and the owner had troubles in keeping in the team some of the best players. This ended up weakening visibly the team: 4 defeats in the first 4 games of the season.

PAUL V. «PITCHIN' PAUL» GOVERNALI

QB
Columbia
1946 Boston Yanks (NFL)
1947 Boston Yanks-New York Giants (NFL)
1948 New York Giants (NFL)
Games: 32; Passing: 218–500, yards 3,348, TDs pass 31, Int. 33; Rushing: 79, yards-83, TDs 4, Fumble 9; Punting: 15, yards 623
1942 All-American
1942 Maxwell Award Player of the Year
1942 All-Ivy League Baseball
COLLEGE FOOTBALL HALL OF FAME

A college career in the Ivy League, always in the spotlight, often on the newspapers of New York; the team of a prestige institution that only a few times in its history has completed a winning season. But this is only a detail: «Pitchin' Paul» enthralls both his fellow players and the faculty in a place where football is just a game, an educative game, but still a game. For him honors and acknowledgements, even in baseball.

In 1946 he reaches the NFL with the new Boston team of the Yanks put together by a singers manager more interested in the tax aspect of the venture than in the results—and in the 3 years the Yanks will survive there will be no other profit … Yet Governali assures the team a solid passing game, with only a few quick retreats and some fumbles too many. His season will end with with a booty of 1,293 yards (the fourth best result among the league's QBs) and the team squarely at the lowest rank of the division with a record of 2–8–1.

In 1947 the Yanks change coach and improve their game; after 4 games Governali moves to the New York Giants that have ended the previous years' Championship with some banned players. Paul will lead the team in the last 8 games, earning a place among the 4 top passers of the NFL. He surely paid back his money, but could not save the Giants from a season to forget. The only satisfaction is the 35–31 victory against the Cardinals, ranked first in the Western and NFL Champions at end season.

In 1948 coach Steve Owen launches a young QB bought from the Redskins, the skilled passer Charlie Conerly, and introduces the T-formation; for Governali remain a few downs and some good punts. It is time to get aside.

After his retirement, we find him as an assistant coach of Lou Little at the Columbia (1949–1956); from the end of the 50s he will be a teacher of athletics for the San Diego State University.

MARIO GRANDINETTI

B
?
1940 Wilmington Clippers (AA)

One trial season with the Clippers.

JOE GRECO

G
Bucknell
1940 Paterson Panthers (AA)

A presence with a modest yield in the farm club of the Chicago Bears

VINCENT GRAVANO (GROVANO)

C
North Carolina State
1942 Long Island Clippers (AA)

He too a teammate of Ken Strong.

ANTHONY S. «TONY» IPPOLITO

G-LB
Purdue
1943 Chicago Bears (NFL)
Games: 9, Int. 1
1943 NFL Western Division Title
1943 NFL Champion

He was a pillar of the Purdue team, rich of talents and ready to pick important results.

In 1943 Tony enters the NFL through the main door: the Bears. With the team of Chicago he is a champion of the division and gains his own personal ticket for the event due on the 26th of December: he disputes the NFL Championship against Washington and «graduates» World Champion». He has reached the top in a few months, but then he has to come down immediately and leave for the military service. In Italy they would say: «*A me mi ha rovinato la guerra …*» («*It was the war that ruined me*»).

DOM IZZO

B
None
1948 Paterson Panthers (AFL)
1948 AFL Playoffs
1948 AFL Title

A 225 lbs. player useful in the middle of the battle. He will be able to boast an AFL title.

VALERIO J. «VAL» «BLACKIE» JANSANTE [GIANSANTE]

OE-DE
Duquesne-Villanova
1946 Pittsburgh Steelers (NFL)
1947 Pittsburgh Steelers (NFL)
1948 Pittsburgh Steelers (NFL)
1949 Pittsburgh Steelers (NFL)
1950 Pittsburgh Steelers (NFL)
1951 Pittsburgh Steelers—Green Bay Packers (NFL)
Games: 68; Receiving: 155, yards 2,356; KRt.: 5, yards 88; 1 Safety Score

A good college career for Val, whose surname acquires an American «J» instead than the Italian «G». Then a discrete wait in the NFL. He will play for 6 years among the pros, highlighting himself as a valid receiver and an aggressive defensive end. Two 2nd rankings in the Division were the best results of his teams.

JOE LA MANNA

HB
NYU
1941 Churchill Pros (AA-Independent)

He is in the roster of the Spingfield team.

NICK LANZA

E
Rice
None.
1948 Blue-Gray Game

A strong player with the Owls towards the end of the 40s.

SAM LAPOLLA

HB
Penn Military
1946 Wilmington Clippers (AFL)

Another prospect come from the military college of Pennsylvania. Not often used by the coaching staff.

ROCCO LA SALA

G
St.Anselm's
1940 Providence Steamrollers (AA)

A bite and run season in Providence, with low results.

JOHN LASCARI

E
Georgetown
1946 Jersey City Giants (AFL)
1946 AFL Title

He plays a good season in the AFL realising a good series of receivings (7 for 176 yards in his first 6 games).

DANTE B. «GLUESFINGER» «SPUMONI» LAVELLI

E
Ohio State
1946 Cleveland Browns (AAFC)
1947 Cleveland Browns (AAFC)
1948 Cleveland Browns (AAFC)
1949 Cleveland Browns (AAFC)
1950 Cleveland Browns (NFL)

1951 Cleveland Browns (NFL)
1952 Cleveland Browns (NFL)
1953 Cleveland Browns (NFL)
1954 Cleveland Browns (NFL)
1955 Cleveland Browns (NFL)
1956 Cleveland Browns (NFL)
Games (AAFC): 44, Rec. 142, Yards 2,580, TDs 29
Games (NFL): 79, Rec. 244, Yards 3,908, TDs 33
1946 AAFC West Division Title
1946 AAFC Champion *(Champ. Game Stats: Rec.6, Yards 87, TD 1)*
1946 ALL-AAFC
1947 AAFC West Division Title
1947 AAFC Champion *(Rec. 3, yards 37)*
1947 ALL-AAFC
1948 AAFC West Division Title
1948 AAFC Champion *(Rec.2, yards 16)*
1949 AAFC Champion *(Rec. 4, yards 56)*
1950 NFL American Conference Title
1950 NFL Champion *(NFL Champ. Game Stats : 2 TDs)*
1951 NFL American Conference Title
1951 NFL Championship Game *(Rec. 4, yards 68)*
1951 NFL All-Pros
1952 NFL American Conference Title
1952 NFL Championship Game *(Rec. 4, yards 23)*
1952 Pro Bowl
1953 NFL American Conference Title
1953 NFL Championship Game *(Rec. 1, yards 13)*
1953 NFL All-Pros
1954 NFL NFL American Conference Title
1954 NFL Champion *(Rec. 1, yards 6)*
1954 Pro Bowl
1955 NFL American Conference Title
1955 NFL Champion *(Rec. 3, yards 95, TD 1)*
1955 Pro Bowl
1940s ALL-PRO SQUAD
PRO FOOTBALL HALL OF FAME

The son of an hammersmith, Angelo, and a housewife, Emily, Dante Lavelli plays baseball and football in high-school when coach Paul Brown (then head-coach at Ohio State, just before becoming one of the major protagonists of the the next thirty years of pro football) picks him up; he will manage to play only few games in the college team, as he first gets injured and then is called to duty in the infantry; he will combat in France, Belgium and Germany before coming back to the normality of football. In 1946 Dante signs up for Paul Brown's new team, in the newborn AAFC: two challenges to the NFL egemony. In the four years the new league stays independent, «Spumoni» (one of the nick-names his teammates have given him) will reveal himself as one of the most shining stars: best receiver in 1946, second and third best in 1947 and 1948, number one again in 1949; and, as a side dish, four victories in the AAFC finals. After 1950 fusion, «Gluesfinger» Lavelli, Paul Brown and the Browns confirm their high profile winning straightaway one conference title and the NFL ring, with Lavelli scoring 2 touchdowns against the Rams. From 1951 to 1956 the «firm» will win 5 division titles and will play 5 NFL finals, winning 2 more; for «Spumoni» the All-Pro nominations are 3. After quitting football Lavelli will settle in Rocky Ridge, Ohio, where he will open a furniture warehouse; he is often in travel for a convention or to sign collectors' cards.

AUGOSTINO SALVATORE «AUGIE» LIO

G-LB
Georgetown
1941 Detroit Lions (NFL)
1942 Detroit Lions (NFL)
1943 Detroit Lions (NFL)
1944 Boston Yanks (NFL)
1945 Boston Yanks (NFL)
1946 Philaldephia Eagles (NFL)
1947 Baltimore Colts (AAFC)
1948 Paterson Panthers (AFL) player—line coach
1949 Paterson Panthers (AFL) player—head coach
Games: 62; Int. 10; PAT 90–95; FGs 6–11; Points 144(NFL)
Games: 10; PATs 19–20; FGs 3–8; Points 28 (AAFC)
Games: 25; PATs 50–53; FGs 14; Points 92 (AFL)
1940 All-American

1940 Orange Bowl
1941 College All-Stars Game
1946 Eagles Top Scorer
1948 AFL Playoffs
1948 AFL Title
1949 AFL Playoffs
1949 AFL Championship Game
1948 AFL All-League Team
All-Time Team Orange Bowl
All-Jersey High School Football Century's Best Players
COLLEGE FOOTBALL HALL OF FAME

The great (and heavy) Augie, already in the spotlight at Passaic High, arrives to Georgetown in the autumn of 1938 and in the same season shows his talent of decisive blocker and precise placekicker; he also demonstrates he likes the battles of the special teams. With the Hoyas he will know a winning streak of 23 games; in 1940 he is the captain of the team which will dispute the Orange Bowl (a controversial, small-measure defeat for 14–7 against Mississippi State). Lio lands to the NFL in 1941; he plays with the Lions together with Whizzer White, an ace who will leave at the end of the season but will later arrive to the Supreme Court.

The team of Detroit plays in 1942 a delusive tournament (0–11–0), with Lio realising 5 out of the 38 points of the whole season.

The things will get better in 1943 with the arrival of a new head-coach and a high quality first choice (Frank Sinkwich); for Augie Lio the seasonal bounty will be of 27 points. Yet the guard will not stay in Detroit to pick the fruits of the growth, because in 944 he will answer to the call of the Boston Yanks, the new team born near home. Another season uphill for 235 lbs. player: the second last ranking in the division and only 16 points. In 1945 the team will repeat the performance of 1944, but Augie will register a total of 27 points.

Then comes 1946: new year, new life. Lio signs for the winning team of the Eagles and by the end of the season has gained 51 points: he is the best scorer for the team of Philadelphia. The last coins of his career will be spent in the AAFC, playing for the Baltimora Colts, a team built around a core of NFL veterans. Nothing of unforgettable, but still Augie Lio brings home 28 points; he is the second scorer of his team. More coins he will then spend with satisfaction in the AFL, with the double role of player and coach: two finals in a row and one victory (2 FGs and 2 PATs in the winning game against the Wilmington Clippers in 1948; 2 PATs in the defeat of 1949 against the Richmond Rebels).

DOMENIC «NICK» LIOTTA

G
Villanova
None
1949 All-American

A cool player. He is one of the pillars of the 1949 team (13th in the national ranking with a record of 8–1–0).

T.A. LOMBARDO

G
Army
None

1944 team captain.

HARRY LORUSSO

G
Temple
1941 Wilmington Clippers (AA)

He plays in the farm club of the Philadelphia Eagles winning the 1941 title.

ED LOVUOLO

T
None
1948 Wilmington Clippers (AFL)
1948 AFL Playoffs

1948 AFL Championship Game

240 pounds on the AFL lines.

FRANK A. LOVUOLO

OE-DE
St.Bonaventure
1949 New York Giants (NFL)
Games: 11; Rec.2, Yards 37; TD 1; Points 6

Frank LoVuolo plays with the New York team two years after the bans linked to the NFL finals. Coach Owen goes on adding new forces and the Giants climb back to the top. LoVuolo is an honest player but does not make the difference.

JOE «CONZY» LUCCI

HB
Youngstown State
1949 Erie Vets (AFL-Independent)

An athlete of discrete fame in college, he will play some games in the independent team of the Vets.

ACHILLE F. «CHICK» MAGGIOLI

DB-HB
Indiana-Notre Dame-Illinois
1948 Buffalo Bills (AAFC)
1949 Detroit Lions (NFL)
1950 Baltimore Colts (NFL)
Games: 7; Rush. 11, yards 27; Rec. 3, yards 23; KRt. 2, yards 38; Punt 2, yards 95;
Int. 1, yards 7 (AAFC)
Games 20; Int. 11, Yards 211, TD 1 (NFL)
High School All-State Football Eleven
1943 NCAA National Championship

1946 NCAA BigTen Championship
1948 NCAA East Division Title
1948 NCAA Championship Game
Indiana Football Hall of Fame

He is famous for having played in 3 different colleges, winning titles with 2 of them. He begins with Indiana but then, because of the war, in 1943 he moves to the Marine Corps Officers Training Program and is redirected to Notre Dame. With the team led by Frank Leahy he gets the national championship.

During the season 1944 Maggioli is called on duty and leaves for the war. When the war ends he resumes his studied at the University of Illinois, where arrives his conference title.

In the AAFC draft of 1948 Maggioli will be chosen by the Buffalo team; with the Bills he will dispute the season acting a bit like a filler, used now and then in the most different roles. For the Bills will arrive the Division title and the league finals; on the 19th of December in Cleveland they will undergo a sound defeat against the mighty Browns. Maggioli, anyway, will get in the record book of the game for an intercept.

In 1949 he moves to the Detroit Lions, where he is displayed as a defensive back (3 intercepts in a season).

In 1950 will be the time of another team: the Baltimore Colts, in the NFL National Conference. Here too Maggioli will be used as a defensive back in his last season.

JOSEPH S. JR. MAGLIOLO

LB
Texas
1948 New York Yankees (AAFC)
Games: 13; Int. 1, 12 yards

One single season among the pros in a middle chart team.

DANTE A. MAGNANI

HB-DB-WB
St.Mary's
1940 Cleveland Rams (NFL)
1941 Cleveland Rams (NFL)
1942 Cleveland Rams (NFL)
1943 Chicago Bears (NFL)
1946 Chicago Bears (NFL)
1947 Los Angeles Rams (NFL)
1948 Los Angeles Rams (NFL)
1949 Chicago Bears (NFL)
1950 Detroit Lions (NFL)
Games: 84; Rush. 331, yards 1,466, TDs 3; Rec. 79; yards 942, TDs 10; Int. 8,
yards 123; PRt. 11, yards 121; KRt. 37, yards 947, TDs 11; Total Points 150
1943 NFL Western Division Title
1943 NFL Champion
1946 NFL Western Division Title
1946 NFL Champion

Starter fullback of the Gaels at St.Mary's (one of the College Top 20s of 1938) he debuts in the NFL in 1940 in a second level team; in 1941 he becomes the big hope of the Rams when during the first game of the season he returns a kickoff to TD with a 95 yards run!

Nothing to do: in the end the Rams will count 2 victories and 8 defeats.

In 1942 Dante is the best scorer of his team with 30 points and in 1943 changes place signing with the Bears. He will be one of the protagonists of the 26th December NFL Champioship Game; during the game he realizes 2 TDs receiving 36 and 66 yards passes from Luckman in the third quarter.

After two years serving his Country in the war (he fights in Guam), Magnani is back to playing with satisfaction: once more a «world champion» in the finals against the NY Giants, when he also scores a TD. In 1947 he moves to California, where he wears again the helmet of the Rams moved to Los Angeles. Magnani will remain on the West Coast ofr two years, playing as a runner, receiver, punt and kickoff returner.

In 1949 he gets back to the Bears; in the meanwhile the Rams have grown visibly, also thanks to coach Shaughnessy and to his playing schemes, and will steal the Bears the Division title.

Dante makes it just in time to play in the new NFL that has incorporated the AAFC and organized two new conferences. He disputes his last pro season with the Detroit Lions, a valuable team led by QB Bobby Laine and the multitalented Doak Walker and packed with experienced «oldies».

Magnani was included in the football cards of the late 40s.

MICHAEL P. MANDARINO

C-G-T
LaSalle
1944 Philadelphia Eagles (NFL)
1945 Philadelphia Eagles (NFL)
1946 Wilmington Clippers (AFL)
1947 Wilmington Clippers (AFL)
Games: 13(NFL)

A valid center grown in the schools of the Philadelphia, Mandarino arrives to the pro team of the city. His debut is in the 1944 NFL championship; with his weight of 240 lbs. he is the biggest player of the Eagles, together with Bucko Kilroy. He will play 2 entire seasons with the team coached by Grease Nealy; Phila will reach both times 2nd in its division. Later Mandarino will play 2 years as a protagonist in the AFL.

RAY MANTONE

T
Villanova
None

On of the regular players of the strong team of Villanova in 1949.

BAPTIST J. «BAP» MANZINI

C-LB
St. Vincent
1944 Phialdelphia Eagles (NFL)
1945 Philadelphia Eagles (NFL)
1948 Philadelphia Eagles-Detroit Lions (NFL)
Games: 23, Int. 1, yards 16

He plays with the Eagles two good seasons, 1944 (1 intercept) and 1945, playing in one of the best defensive lines of the league and gaining the 2nd place in the Eastern Division (7–1–2 and 7–3–0 the seasonal records). In 1948 Bap plays his part in the beginning of the winning season of the Eagles (division title and then NFL champions), but at the half of the championship moves to Detroit to help the new owner in the task of rebuilding the Lions.

JOSEPH M. «JOE» MANZO

T
Boston College
1945 Detroit Lions (NFL)
Games : 3
1940 Cotton Bowl
1941 Sugar Bowl
Boston College Varsity Club Athletic Hall of Fame

A college football star (graduated in 1941) and one of the strongest tackles of Boston College, winner of both the Cotton and the Sugar Bowl.

In his curriculum also one season in the NFL.

BASILIO MARCHI

G-C-LB
New York Univ.
1934 Pittsburgh Pirates (NFL)
1942 Philadelphia Eagles (NFL)

Games: 12

The tawny Basilio (216 lbs.) makes his debut at 25 in the half 30s NFL. His team knows little results. 8 years later, aged 33, he is called by the Eagles; he is «grown» some more reaching the 225 lbs. At the age of 34 he will be called also by the Army for three whole years (1943–1945).

HUGO F. MARCOLINI

WB-DB
St.Bonaventure
1948 Brooklyn Dodgers (AAFC)
Games: 10; Rush. 5, yards 11; Rec. 2, yards 38; KRt. 2, yards 33

He plays with the twin team of the baseball franchise (the owners are the same). A season to forget at Ebbets Fields; by the half of the season there will be a merger with the Yankees.

JOSEPH A. «JOE» «WHITE BRITCHES» MARGUCCI

WB-QB-HB-DB
USC
1947 Detroit Lions (NFL)
1948 Detroit Lions (NFL)
Games : 22 ; Rushing 60, yards 111, TDs 4 ; Rec. 46, yards 575, TDs 3; KRt. 15, yards 293; PRt. 12, yards 123
1945 Pacific Coast Conf. Title
1945 Rose Bowl

Here is a physically huge player who after a good college career arrives among the pros full of expectations. Here is a player who knows how to do everything and is often cornered by some specialist, so he passes, runs, receives, returns and does not remain in the annals.

JOE MARINO

T
William & Mary
1942 Long Island Clippers (AA)

A good athlete, much valued at college, present in the roster of the Clippers.

VIC MARINO

G
Ohio State
1940 Boston Bears (AFL)
1941 New York Americans (AFL)
1946 Akron Bears (AFL)
1940 AFL All-League Team

A good AFL player in 1940–1941, one of the most respceted athletes of Fenway Park in Boston. A bit less at the Yankee Stadium. In 1946 we find him in the new edition of the AFL, this time at Akron, in a team owned by the Chicago Bears.

JOHNNY MARIUCCI

E
Minnesota
1941 Churchill Pros (AA-Independent)

A quick passage in the team tat plays its home games at the Pynchon Park of Springfield.

SALVATORE J. «SAL» MARONE

G
Manhattan
1943 New York Giants (NFL)
Games: 8

He plays one season together with Al Blozis and Mel Hein. Something to remember for the whole life. The Giants end 2nd in the division (6–3–1).

LOUIS «LOU» MAROTTI

G-E
Toledo
1940 Cincinnati Bengals (AFL)
1941 Long Island Indians (AA)
1943 Chicago Cardinals (NFL)
1944 Chicago Cardinals-Pittsburgh Steelers (NFL)
1945 Chicago Cardinals (NFL)
Games: 15; KRt. 1(NFL)

Marotti debuts among the pros in the AFL, in a team decimated by the injuries.

After a passage in the American League it is the turn of another difficult debut in the NFL, with a team always losing.

The following year he plays with a team the press baptizes «the Carpets» (0–10–0). 1945 is his last season as a pro, and the Cards are still last of the list, even though they are slowly rebuilding the team; Marotti will not be there to pick the results.

PASQUALE J. «PATSY» MARTINELLI

C-LB
Scranton
1941 Wilmington Clippers (AA)
1942 Wilmington Clippers (AA)
1946 Buffalo Bisons (AAFC)
1946 Scranton Miners-Wilmington Clippers (AFL)
1947 Wilmington Clippers (AFL)
1948 Wilmington Clippers (AFL)
1949 Wilmington Clippers (AFL)
Games: 3, Int. 1, yards 12(AAFC)
1941 AA All-League Team (AA)

1941 AA Title
1948 AFL Playoffs
1948 AFL Championship

He debuts in the American Association with the Clippers that win the 1941 title.

Later, after the war, Patsy will be on of the rookies of the new AAFC league; a team from Buffalo trying to get back on the pro circus after the attempts of the 20s (Buffalo All-Americans) and of the early 40a (in the American Football League).

After 3 games he gest back home to play for the Miners, then again with the Clippers in the American Football League: another coming back. He will stay in Wilmington for three years, with more than one satisfaction.

LEONARD L. «LEN» MASINI

FB-LB
Fresno State
1947 S.Francisco 49ers (AAFC)
1948 S.Francisco 49ers-Los Angeles Dons (AAFC)
Games : 24 ; Rush. 41, yards 179, TDs 2; Int. 1

After a good season in Fresno, Masini lands to the 49ers; the team is competitive (8–4–2) and ends the season behind the strongest Browns. Len scores 2 TDs and 1 defensive intercept. The second pro season is spent between San Francisco and Los Angeles; with the Dons he will be on field for one of his last AAFC games.

AL MASTRANGELI

C
Illinois
None.
1949 College All-Stars Game

A leading player in the last 40s for Illinois.

JOHN BATTISTA MASTRANGELO

G-T-LB
Notre Dame
1947 Pittsburgh Steelers (NFL)
1948 Pittsburgh Steelers (NFL)
1949 New York Yankees(AAFC)
1950 New York Giants (NFL)
Games: 32(NFL); 12 (AAFC)
1945, 1946 All-American
1947 Chicago College All-Stars Game

Returned back home by the Army for some sight problem, John Battista becomes a strong player for Notre Dame in the last years of the war; he was one of the first athletes of high level to wear contact lenses during a game. Between 1944 and 1946, from reserve lineman becomes in the turn of few months a national level player, contributing to the amazing 1946 season of the Irish (1st in the national ranking).

Chosen in the 2nd round of the 1947 draft by Pittsburgh, he debuts straightaway in the NFL, playing 11 games out of 12; the Steelers (8–4–0) end 2nd in their division.

1948 is a tragic year for his team: coach Sutherland suddenly falls badly ill and the team results are disastrous; Mastrangelo will play all the games trying to do his duty at best.

In 1949 he decides to change life and signs for an AAFC franchise in New York, the Yankees. There he plays with a young defensive back, a rookie named Tom Landry ...

He ends his pro career in the same city, but at a different address: the Giants. Just in time to play a season in the new NFL with the new conferences configuration.

He appears in the 1949 Bowman cards collection.

FRED «BUTCH» MASTRIOLA

G-E
North Carolina State
1940 Boston Bears (AFL)
1941 Providence Steamrollers (AA)

He plays only one season in the AFL with the team led by Eddie Casey; Boston is the 3rd force of the chiampionship and will end the season with a 5–4–1 record. In 1941 he will move to Providence (American Association) but only for a short experience, after which he will leave the pro world.

JOHN B. MATISI

T
Duquesne
1943 Brooklyn Dodgers (NFL)
Inserire AAFC TEAM
Games: 4; Int. 1 (NFL); Games: 12 (AAFC)

He arrives to the NFL aged 22, chosen in the 7th round of the draft; with the Brooklyn team he will only play 4 games, realising 1 intercept. After 2 years of war he is back home to receive the call from Buffalo; he will play one single season in the AAFC.

FRANCIS A. «FRANK» MATTIOLI

G-LB
Pittsburgh
1946 Pittsburgh Steelers (NFL)
Games: 11

A quick sports career consumed in the Pittsburgh area, first in college and then among the pros: one season with the Steelers.

BEN MAUCERI

E
NYU
1941 Churchill Pros (AA-Independent)

In the roster of the Springfield team.

VINCENT L. «VINCE» MAZZA

DE-OE
none
1945 Detroit Lions (NFL)
1946 Detroit Lions (NFL)
1947 Buffalo Bills (AAFC)
1948 Buffalo Bills (AAFC)
1949 Buffalo Bills (AAFC)
Games: 6 (NFL);
Games: 39; Rec. 2, yards 11, TD 1; Int. 1, 32 yards (AAFC)
1948 AAFC East Division Title
1948 AAFC Championship Game

A winning debut in the NFL for the tall and strong Vince, displayed in defense. In 1947 he finds a better contract in the new league and so signs with Buffalo. In the Bills (this is the new name of the former «Bisons») he will play three regular years, most often in defense but sometimes also in offense. In 1948 he will dispute the AAFC finals, defeated bt the amazing Cleveland Browns in their perfect season.

HARRY MAZZEI

QB-HB-K
Villanova
1940 Long Island Indians (AA)
1941 Long Island Indians (AA)
1940 AA Playoffs

Leading player in 1938 at Villanova (team record: 8–0–1).

In 1940 he lands to the American Association realising 16 points: he is the seasonal top scorer for the team linked to the Detroit Lions. Sam story in 1941 (6th best scorer in the league) with 3 TDs and 5 PATs.

ARCH MILANO

E-DE
St.Francis
1945 Detroit Lions (NFL)
Games :1

A light mark in the NFL, only one game played with the Detroit team.

FRANK D. MININI

HB-FB-DB
San Jose State
1947 Chicago Bears (NFL)
1948 Chicago Bears (NFL)
1949 Pittsburgh Steelers (NFL)
Games: 36; Rush. 51, yards 216, TDs 4; Rec. 3, yards 37, TD 1; KRt. 39, yards 1,021, TD 1; Int. 1
1946 Raisin Bowl

After a nice experience with the Spartans of San Jose and after 42 months in the war (he fought in the Philippines and on the Solomon Islands), Minini is put under contract by the Bears.

He is an athlete with a good size and a good technique who manages to find some space among many champions. In 1949 he is on the Bowman cards.

ANTHONY S. «SKIPPY» MINISI

HB-DB
Pennsylvania, Navy
1948 New York Giants (NFL)
Games: 12; Rush. 36, yards 160, TD 1, Rec. 13, yards 123, TD 1; PRt. 3, yards 25;
KRt. 4, yards 82; Int. 2
1946 All-American
1946,1947 Ivy League Title
COLLEGE FOOTBALL HALL OF FAME

After the high school at Newark Academy, Skippy goes on to study and play at Penn; he will be transferred to the Navy for one year (1945), then he will be back to Penn, where he will become a star running back and an All-American.

In the college games he is often decisive, a true leader.

In this period he scores 17 TDs, rushing 170 times for 840 yards and completing 60 of 82 passes for 562 yards.

First choice of the Giants, he will play for one season in the NFL before becoming senior partner of an importante law firm of Philadelphia and the president of the Association of Intercollegiate Football Officials. In 30 years Minisi will officiate in over 100 major college games.

RAYMOND W. «RAY» MONACO

G-LB
Holy Cross
1941 Providence Steamrollers (AA)—Churchil Pros(AA-Independent)
1944 Washington Redskins (NFL)
1945 Cleveland Rams (NFL)
Games: 6 (NFL)
1945 NFL Eastern Division Title

Monaco will play 5 games in his first NFL season, ranking 3rd in his division with the Redskins (6–3–1 their record).

Not remarkable his second year as a pro: he will get injured but the team will win the divisional title anyway.

SAM MONACO

E
Villanova
1940 Newark Bears (AA)

An interesting college career; a quick ride on the rollercoaster of the farm clubs.

RUSS MONICA

G
Fordham
1946 Newark Bombers (AFL)

A 32 years old athlete who manages to find some room in the AFL.

JOHN MORELLI

LB
Georgetown
1944 Boston Yanks (NFL)
1945 Boston Yanks (NFL)
Games : 19; 2 TDs, Int.1

In his first year as a pro, although playing for a disastrous team, he manages to score 2 TDs!

Also in 1945 he shows good things, with many valid actions in defense and 1 intercept.

ALFRED V. MORRO

DT-OT
Boston College
None.
1940 Cotton Bowl
1941 Sugar Bowl
1941 Boston College Captain
Boston College Varsity Club Athletic Hall of Fame

An offensive and defensive tackle, one of the leaders of the Boston College Eagles. A record of 27–5 with him on field.

Apatr from the successes on the gridiron, Morro was also a USA National Junior Discus Champion and record-holder, 3rd nationwide as a senior.

PAUL MORTELLARO

T
Florida
1949 Erie Vets (AFL-Independent)

Another Florida player arrived to the Vets in search for luck.

ANTHONY «TONY» ORSINI

RB
Scranton
None.
1948 Middle Atlantic Conference Title
1949 Middle Atlantic Conference Title
1948 All-Pennsylvania
New Jersey Coaches Hall of Fame

A starter at Scranton from 1946–1949 (record 21–16–1); he led the team in rushing all four years and won two conferences titles.

Before dedicating with success to a career of football coaching, he took part to many try-outs with NFL teams (Rams, Colts, 49ers), with discrete prospectives but little luck.

MIKE OSTINATO

G
Georgetown
None
1940 Orange Bowl

One of the points of strength of the college in 1939 (7–0–1) and 1940 (8–2–0).

CLIFFORD E. PACE

E
Rhode Island
None.
Rhode Island Athletics Hall of Fame

A true local hero, an athlete excelling in football, baseball and basketball in the late 1930s and early 40s.

During the war he will be a Commander in the U.S. Coast Guard; later he will become a good golf player, a successful businessman and a leader in his community.

LOUIS J. «LOU» PALAZZI

C-LB
Penn State
1946 New York Giants (NFL)
1947 New York Giants (NFL)
Games: 16
1946 NFL Eastern Division Title
1946 NFL Championship Game

After a discrete college career, Lou is chosen in the 5th round of the Giants, a team in search of rebirth. The season is successful, Lou is a starter in 5 games and gains a ticket for the finals.

The party will be ruined by a ban of the league to 2 Giants athletes.

In 1947 Palazzi will play 11 games in a team that has definitely lost its bearings.

NICK PALAZZI

HB
?
1941 Churchill Pros (AA-Independent)

In the roster of the team that hired the athletes of Providence after the Steamrollers abandoned.

ROBERT «BOB» PALLADINO

B
Notre Dame
None.

A good player of the Irish of Notre Dame, led by Frank Leahy.

In 1947 he is chosen in the 25th round of the NFL draft by the Green Bay Packers.

He will never get on the field with the pros.

VIC PALLADINO

G
Boston College
None.
1942 Lambert Trophy
1942 Orange Bowl

1947 All-New England Team
1948 All-East
Boston College Varsity Club Athletic Hall of Fame.

An outstanding sophomore guard who leads the Boston College Eagles in a great season culminating with the unlucky game against Alabama in the Orange Bowl.

After the break of the war the college resumes the normal activities and Vic is successfully back in the midfield.

In 1947 he will be the recipient of the first edition of the Thomas F. Scanlon Award (*Scholar, Athlete, Gentleman and Friend*).

LAWRENCE R. PANCIERA

LB
Rhode Island
None.
Rhode Island Athletic Hall of Fame

Rams football and baseball star at Rhode Island State College in the mid of 40s.

Later he will become one of the New England most successful baseball coaches ever.

JOSEPH «JOE» PAPIANO

FB-K
Temple
1948 Wilmington Clippers (AFL)
1949 Wilmington Clippers (AFL)
1948 AFL Playoffs
1948 AFL Championship Game

After gaining the spotlight at Temple, Papiano arrives to the AFL and immediately confirms himself as a skilled athlete; he ends his first season as the 5th best runner in the league (82 carryings for 402 yards and 5 TDs) and as the 3rd best scorer with 44 points. In the post season he takes part to the playoffs (22–14 against the Richmond Rebels, 1 FG and 3 PATs for him) and arrives to the Championship Game, where the team id defeated 24–14 by the Paterson Panthers. In this game Papiano kicks 2 PATs

ALFRED «FRED» PASCALE

T
Mt. St.Mary's
1941 New York Yankees (AA)

He gets to the American Association with the new team of Douglas Hertz, who had already owned a franchise with the same name in the AFL.

JOSEPH B. «JOE» PASQUA

T
SMU
1942 Cleveland Rams (NFL)
1943 Washington Redskins (NFL)
1946 Los Angeles Rams (NFL)
Games: 24; PATs 2–2
1940 NCAA SWC Title
1943 NFL Eastern Division Title
1943 NFL Championship Game

After the lucky 1940 season with the Southern Methodist team, Pasqua lands to the NFL; he debuts positively with the Rams playing 11 games and realizing 1 PAT. At the end of the season the Redskins dispute the NFL finals against the; Pasqua has no chance to kick a PAT.

The Rams will be defeated by the Bears with a heavy difference (41–21).

After the war he will join the new Rams in the West Coast to dispute another season. 4 games for a goodbye.

JOE PATANELLI

T-K
Indiana
None.
Indiana Hall of Fame

Gratuated in 1942, he tries the Chicago Cards and then is called by the Army. Joe also played professional basketball, baseball and was a heavyweight boxer.

MICHAEL J. «MIKE» «SUPERMAN» PATANELLI

DE
Bowling Green State, Ball State
1947 Brooklyn Dodgers (AAFC)

One of the many Patanelli from Indiana who fight in the winter football fields. One single season with the pros under the lead of the former star Cliff Battles.

ANGELO PATERNOSTER

G-LB
?
1943 Washington Redskins (NFL)
1943 Eastern Division Title
1943 NFL Championship Game

A short experience in the NFL, crowned with a divisional title and a quick appearance in the finals lost to the Bears.

JOSEPH F. «FRANK» PERANTONI

G
Princeton
1948 New York Yankees (AAFC)
1949 New York Yankees (AAFC)

Games: 28

He debuts among the pros in a team shaken by the change of the coaches; Peran-toni, anyway, is a young starter center. Definitely better the 1949 season, ended with a positive record (8–4–0); the Yankees will display on the field one of the best offensive lines in the league. And Perantoni was there.

ROBERT I. «BOB» PERINA

DB-RB-HB
Princeton
1946 New York Yankees (AAFC)
1947 Brooklyn Dodgers (AAFC)
1948 Chicago Rockets (AAFC)
1949 Chicago Bears (NFL)
1950 Baltimore Colts (NFL)
Games: 40; Passing: 32–72, yards 380, TD 1; Rushing: 118, yards 252, TDs 4; Interception: 12, yards 151 (AAFC).
Games: 13; Rush.: 4, yards 4; Rec.: 3, yards 33; Int.: 6, yards 23; KRt.: 1, yards 11 (NFL)
1946 AAFC East Division Title
1946 AAFC Championship Game

A player for every season, used as a QB, a runner, a defensive back and a receiver. A career that saw Perini playing in both the pro leagues, from the divisional title in 1946 to the AAFC finals (lost to the unbeatable Cleveland Browns), from the slums (the years with the Dodgers and the Rockets) back to the first line with the contract offered him by the Bears. He will end as the Colts vet in the new enlarged NFL.

In his career as a defensive liner Perini completed 18 intercepts.

MICHAEL A. «MIKE» PERROTTI

T
Ohio State
1948 Los Angeles Dons (AAFC)

1949 Los Angeles Dons (AAFC)
Games : 26

After showing his talent with the Ohio State Buckeyes, Perrotti obtains an AAFC contract on the West Coast, in the Lindheimer team that has spent loads of money to hire promising champions (apart from Perrotti will arrive two great players like Herm Wedemeyer and Len Ford).

The owner's efforts notwithstanding, the team will not escape mediocrity and will melt away. At the end of the season Perrotti's pro career is over.

JOHN A. «PEPPER» PETRELLA

HB-DB
Penn State
1945 Pittsburgh Steelers (NFL)
1949 Bethlehem Bulldogs (AFL)
Games: 3; Rush.: 15, yards 33, PRt.: 6, yards 52; KRt.: 3, yards 85; Int. 1, yards 8 (NFL)
1949 AFL Playoffs

Petrella is a good player at Penn State. In 1945 he plays his cards in the NFL. He is not lucky. He will play 3 games, performing a couple of significant returns and gaining a respectable amount of yards. In 1949 we find him in the AFL, where he makes it to the record book realizing 2 TDs and a dozen of good runs.

WILLIAM J. «BILL» PICCOLO

C-T
Canisius
1943 New York Giants (NFL)
1944 New York Giants (NFL)
1945 New York Giants (NFL)
Games: 18; Int. 2, yards 5; TD 1 Fumble Rec.
1944 NFL Eastern Division Title
1944 NFL Championship Game

Chosen in the 8th round by the NY Giants, he reveals himself a good rookie and plays 10 games of the 1943 season with a good team (2nd in the Eastern division); in the next two years as a pro he will be nothing more than a back-up for a player like Mel Hein.

CAMILLO PICCONE

HB
Notre Dame
1946 Bethlehem Bulldogs (AFL)
1947 Bethlehem Bulldogs (AFL)
1946 AFL All-League Team
1946 AFL Western Division Title
1946 AFL Title
1947 AFL Western Division Title
1947 AFL Title

In 1946 he plays a good season (67 runs for 382 yards and 3 TDs, plus 4 receivings for 172 yards and 2 TDs) and wins the title with the farm club of Philadelphia. He is coached by another paisà, former athlete Enio «Ed» Conti (born in Naples, Italy). Piccone will repeat his good season in 1947, with 7 intercepts.

ROBERT M. SR. «BOB» PIFFERINI

LB-C
San Jose State
1949 Detroit Lions (NFL)
Games : 12 ; Int. 3, yards 3

A star in the defensive line of San Jose State in the golden years 1946–1947 (record: 17–2–1), Pifferini is chosen by Detroit in the 15th draft of the 1949 NFL draft.

A good debut: he will be a starter in all the games of the season, with 3 intercepts. The game is over because of a bad injury.

HENRY W. «WHITEY» «HANK» PIRO

E-DB
Syracuse
1941 Philadelphia Eagles (NFL)
Games: 10; Rec.: 10, yards 141, TDs 1; KRt.: 1. yards 33

Born from a «double immigration»: the grandfather had moved from Southern Italy to Germany and he moved as a child from Northorz, where he was born in 1917, to the States together with his parents. He will leave Syracuse to play with Philadelphia in the NFL. One year, one championship (his arrival coincides with that of Tommy Thompson), and then the war: a journey backwards to help forming the Europa of the future.

ROCCO ALBERTO «ROCKY» PIRRO

G-DB-LB-FB
Catholic
1940 Pittsburgh Steelers (NFL)
1941 Pittsburgh Steelers (NFL)
1942 Worcester Panthers (AA)
1946 Buffalo Bisons (AAFC)
1947 Buffalo Bills (AAFC)
1948 Buffalo Bills (AAFC)
1949 Buffalo Bills (AAFC)
Games: 20; Rush.: 1, yards 1; Rec.: 2, yards 31; Int. 1, 2 yards (NFL).
1940 Sun Bowl
Catholic Hall of Fame
1948 AAFC East Division Title
1948 AAFC Championship Game

Catholic's starting fullback, Pirro is chosen in the 16th round of the 1940 draft by Pittsburgh. Rocky plays 2 seasons with the Steelers, not picking many results.

After a 4 years break caused by the war, Pirro is back to the pro football thanks to a contract with Buffalo (AAFC) In the new league he will know a second sporting youth, disputing 4 seasons as an expert guard and gaining some satisfactions: a

2nd place in the East Division in 1947, a divisional title and the finals in 1948 (defeated by the usual Browns), 2 ties against Cleveland in 1949.

LOU PRESTI

G-C-T
Holy Cross
1941 Hartford Blues (Independent-AA)

A good athlete playing the home games in the Municipal Stadium.

DOMINIC A. «DOM» PRINCIPE

FB-BB-DB-LB
Fordham
1940 New York Giants (NFL)-1941 New York Giants (NFL)
1942 New York Giants (NFL)
1946 Brooklyn Dodgers (AAFC)
Games: 25; Rushing: 12, 13 yards.; Rec. 6, 87 yards.; Int.1(NFL)
Games:10;Rushing: 39, 139 yards, 2 TDs (AAFC).
1939 College All-Star
1941 NFL East Division Title
1941 NFL Cham1pionship Game
Fordham Hall of Fame

He plays in Fordham between 1937 and 1939; in his last year he realizes 7 TDs and is selected for the College All-Stars. Principe is one of the protagonists of the game between the college stars and the NFL champions Green Bay Packers.

In 1940 he is drafted at the 6th round by the NY Giants (NFL). In the years 1940-'41 he plays two good seasons in many roles; in 1941 he is a conference champion. On the 7th of December he is in the Polo Grounds when the speakers summon all the soldiers to their barracks: the attack of Pearl Harbor has begun. On the 21st of December he is in Chicago for the saddest Championship Game in front of less than 13,000 people); the Bears beat the Giants 37–9.

After the military service, at the end of the war, he debuts in the new league in 1946; his coach is Cliff Battles, a famous glory of the Redskins.

Principe was one of the athletes whose career was broken by the war. When he will be back among the pros, after three years spent overseas, he will be 29 years old.

BENITO M. «BEN» PUCCI

T
none
1946 Buffalo Bisons (AAFC)
1947 Chicago Rockets (AAFC)
1948 Cleveland Browns (AAFC)
Games: 37
1948 AAFC West Division Title
1948 AAFC Champion

A big man (260 lbs.), always the heaviest in all of his teams.

After 2 years fighting for medium-low quality teams, Pucci receives the call from Paul Brown. In his last year as a pro he will pack many satisfactions: one divisional title and one title of the league conquered against his former team (Cleveland-Buffalo 49–7).

PHILIP J. «PHIL» RAGAZZO

T-G
Case Western Reserve
1938 Cleveland Rams (NFL)
1939 Cleveland Rams (NFL)
1940 Cleveland Rams-Philadelphia Eagles (NFL)
1941 Philadelphia Eagles
1945 New York Giants (NFL)
1946 New York Giants (NFL)
1947 New York Giants (NFL)
Games: 63; Int. 1, yards 6

1946 NFL Eastern Division Title
1946 NFL Championship Game
Case Western Reserve University Hall of Fame

Chosen by Green Bay (round 6, draft 1938) and put under contract by Cleveland; 7 years in the NFL, with a 3 years break caused by the war, and many games played with passion and courage. The mature years will also bring him some unhoped results, like the divisional title of 1946.

BENJAMIN L. «BEN» RAIMONDI

TB
William&Mary, Indiana
1947 New York Yankees (AAFC)
1948 Jersey City Giants-Richmond Rebels (AFL)
1949 Richmond Rebels (AFL)
1950 Brooklyn Football Brooks (AFL)
Games: 7; Passing: 3–15, yards 54; Rush.: 6, yards 11(AAFC);
Pass.: 74–161, yards 954, TDs pass 12 (AFL)
1946 All-BigTen
1947 AAFC East Division Title
1947 AAFC Championship Game
1948 AFL Playoffs
1949 AFL Playoffs
1949 AFL Title

A quality career in the college football with the Indiana Hoosiers (4th nationwide in 1945).

In the AAFC he is in fact the back up of strong Spec Sanders. In 1948 he moves to the AFL, where he gains attention as one of the 4 best QBs of the season. He will also reach the playoffs, hitting 1 TD in run and 1 TD on pass in the semifinals.

He will repeat his season in 1949, with the Rebels that end 1st after the regular season; follows a victory in the playoffs and in the AFL Championship Game (his stats: 8–11, 160 yards, 2 TDs passes and 1 XP pass).

The following year he will move to Brooklyn as a QB and an assistant coach.

JOHN «JOHNIE» RIOLA

QB
NTU
None.
1939, 1940 Lone Star Conference Title
1940 All-Conference
1940 Little All-American

Starter QB of the North Texas University in the seasons 1939–1940, Riola is a quality player, the best of the whole conference.

After the college years he will become a good head coach in high school and in 1948 he will win a national title with Waco High.

PETER «PETE» ROBOTTI

T
Connecticut State
1941 Jersey City Giants (AA)
1941 AA Playoffs

A good athlete debuting in the team led by coach Ed Franco.

PAUL ROMANO

HB-DB
Wisconsin
1946 Akron Bears (AFL)
1947 Paterson Panthers (AFL)
Games: 7; TD 1; XP 2–3
1946 AFL Championship Game
1947 AFL Eastern Division Title
1947 AFL Championship Game

In 1946 he hits the AFL titles with a satellite team of the Chicago Bears. In 1947, after gaining the spotlight with 6 intercepts in the course of the regular season he repeats himself and reaches the finals with his new team. Also this time he plays in the losing franchise.

RUDOLPH «RUDY» ROMBOLI

FB-LB
None
1946 Boston Yanks (NFL)
1947 Boston Yanks (NFL)
1948 Boston Yanks (NFL)
Games: 27; Rushing: 49, yards 137, TD 1; Rec.: 12, yards 107; KRt.: 4, yards 86;
Int:: 2, yards 26

Romboli arrives to the NFL with no college experience. He debuts in the team of Ted Collins, in a roster full of paisà (Governali, Famiglietti, Abruzzi, Calcagni, Canale). He has a good athletic mass.

In his second year he is displayed by his coach also in offense and registers a discrete number of carryings. The Yanks leave the last place in the division. Another discrete year for Rudy will be 1948, with some good performances (unforgettable the victory against the Philadelphia Eagles, the best team in the division and an NFL finalist). The transferral of the franchise to New York will coincide with the end of his pro career.

SALVATORE «SAL THE TANK» ROSATO

FB-LB
Villanova
1945 Washington Redskins (NFL)
1946 Washington Redskins (NFL)
1947 Washington Redskins (NFL)
Games: 23; Rush.: 159, yards 620, TDs 4; Rec.: 9, yards 131, TD 1; KRt.: 3, yards 53; PRt.: 1, yards 12
1945 Shrine East-West Game

Sal is a very good athlete already in the high school, where he gains appraisal in football, basketball and track. Later he will be the regular fullback of Villanova; with the Wildcats he will dispute important seasons and will be known nationwide. Good performances also in the NFL; he will become a favourite of the Redskins. His image will be included in the cards of late 40s.

OSCAR ROTATORI

G-C
Rhode Island State
1941 Churcill Pros (AA_Independent)
1946 Bethlehem Bulldogs (AFL)

First a trial as a pro with a Springfield team, then he will become one of the many paisà of the Bulldogs, the farm club of the Eagles. With him Conti, Cippiciani, Dini, Donato, Piccone.

AL ROTELLA

G
Tennessee
None

He played with the Vols in 1942 and in 1946–1947, winning a conference title. Later he will become a high school and college coach. In the 70s his son Jamie will play in Tennessee, becoming team captain in 1972.

MARIO «MAUDE» ROZZONI

G
?
1940 Kenosha Cardinals (AFL)

One of the back-ups of a wide roster. The team is led by John Reis and the player-coach Johnny Blood.

ANTHONY E. «TONY» RUBINO

G
Wake Forest
1943 Detroit Lions (NFL)
1946 Detroit Lions (NFL)
Games : 21

A strong guard at college; with the Demon Deacons of Wake Forest he is a protagonist of the 1942 season (6–2–1). Chosen by the Lions, Rubino disputes 10 in the NFL before leaving for the war.

In 1946 he is back with a team shaken by the loss of important players, passed to the new league: AAFC pays better. It will be a season to forget.

SESTO SANTERILLI

FB-K
Fordham
1947 Wilkes-Barre Barons (AFL)

Coming from the football school of the Rams in Fordham, he plays with the team born after the renounce of the Scranton franchise. Sesto will be the AFL leader for number of punts (48, with an average of 38 yards).

ALEXANDER «ALEX» SANTILLI

T
Fordham
None
1941 Sugar Bowl
Fordham University Hall of Fame

Regular Tackle in the 1941 team. The Rams will end the season 6th in the national ranking with a record of 8–1–0 and a prestigious affirmation in a bowl.

FRANK SANTORA

DB-QB
None
1944 Boston Yanks (NFL)
Games: 1

A quick and mysterious passage in the NFL: no college, no particular aptitude or experience. The only thing we know is that he played football at high school in Garfield, New Jersey. In the league he only plays one game, aged 18! He is the protagonist of a kickoff return of 27 yards, then nothing more.

ALBERTO R. «AL» SANTUCCI

C
Santa Clara
None
Santa Clara University Hall of Fame

Regular center in the 1942 Broncos (record: 7–2–0) led by famous coach Buck Shaw.

DOMINIC F. «MICKEY» SANZOTTA

WB-DB-RB
Case Western Reserve
1942 Detroit Lions (NFL)
1946 Detroit Lions (NFL)
Games : 20 ; Rush. : 77, yards 340; Rec.: 7, yards 35; Passing: 4–16, yards 45; PRt.: 7, yards 87; KRt.: 2, yards 40; Punt: 1, yards 42.

After gaining the spotlight at Case, Sanzotta is chosen by the Lions in the 4th round and arrives to the NFL. A quick experience cut in two by the war. In 1942, anyway, he will be the best runner of his team.

LAWRENCE M. «LARRY» SARTORI

G
Fordham
1942 Detroit Lions (NFL)
1945 Detroit Lions (NFL)
1946 Jersey City Giants (AFL)
1948 Newark Bears (AFL-Independent)
1949 Jersey City Giants (AFL)
Games : 11 ; Punt 1, yards 42 (NFL)
1941 Sugar Bowl
1946 AFL Eastern Division Title
1946 AFL Title

Here is another product of Fordham, protagonist with the Maroons in the big seasons 1939 (6–2–0 and 17th place in the national rank), 1940 (7–2–0 and 12th in the national rank) and 1941 (8–1–0, 8th nationwide and a victorty in the Sugar Bowl).

Also for him the war will mark a fracture in his pro career. Later will follow a passage in the AFL farm clubs, crowned by a title of the league.

JOSEPH «JOE» SARULLO

E
Manhattan
1941 New York Yankees (AA)

A very complicated year with the team of his city.

THEODORE G. «TED» SCALISSI

HB-DB
Ripon
1947 Chicago Rockets (AAFC)
Games: 10; Rush.: 36, yards 37; Rec. 5, yards 67, TDs 2; PRt.: 2, yards 26; KRt.: 8, yards 171

One single season in a failing team (1–13–0), some good receivings, 2 TDs and many valid returns. A very short yet decent career in the NFL; in 1948 he will sign a contract for the basketball league: less injuries and a roof over the field. This way Scalissi enters the strict number of the *Two-Sport Stars* (only a few more than 100 pros in a century!).

RAY SCAPECCHI

B
Monmouth
1940 East Chicago Indians (Independent-AFL)

He plays in an «open» team that now and then hires for a few gams NFL players. Some names: Don Hutson, Parker Hall, George Cafego, Bruiser Kinard. Few dollars and many defeats.

JOE SCARPA

G
Upsala
1946 Newark Bombers (AFL)
1948 Newark Bears (AFL-Independent)

He plays in the AFL in a team of low results (1946 record: 2–7–1). Not much better in 1948.

TONY SCHIRO

G
Santa Clara
None

In 1942 he is highly respectable guard for the Santa Clara Broncos (7–2–0 and 16th in the national ranking).

GEORGE J. SELLA JR.

B
Princeton
1949 All-American

A good player, one of the few to be elected All-American in the history of the Ivy League institution.

FRANK SENO

DB-HB-WB
George Washington
1943 Washington Redskins (NFL)
1944 Washington Redskins (NFL)
1945 Chicago Cardinals (NFL)
1946 Chicago Cardinals (NFL)
1947 Boston Yanks (NFL)
1948 Boston Yanks (NFL)
1949 Washington Redskins (NFL)
Games: 67; Int. 19, yards 160; Rush.: 364, yards 1,292, TDs 2; Rec.: 73, yards 1,034, TDs 5; PRt.: 64, yards 747, TD 1; KRt.: 80, yards 1,916, TD 1
1943 NFL Eastern Division Title
1943 NFL Championship Game

Here is a player who surely left a visible mark in the NFL of the 40s, a polyvalent athlete whose talent is well summed by his numbers:

7 years as a pro, more than 4,000 gained running, receiving, returning, intercepting.

After two years and a divisional title with the Redskins, in 1945 he moves to the Cardinals, immediately revealing himself as one of the best runners of the team; moreover, he will be a formidable returner (more than 800 yards in 2 years). Two years in Chicago and then off to Boston. In his first year with the Yanks he brings home 10 intercepts! By the end of the second year he has returned for more than 800 yards, carried the ball for 456 and received for 440.

At the end of his career he is back to Washington, where in the 1949 season he will be displayed as a defensive back. While he is there he will also complete 2 kickoff returns for 39 yards.

DOMENICO «DOM» SIGILLO

T
Xavier (Ohio)
1937 Cincinnati Bengals (AFL)
1938 Cincinnati Bengals (Ind.—AFL)
1939 Columbus Bullies (AFL)
1940 Columbus Bullies (AFL)
1941 Columbus Bullies (AFL)
1943 Chicago Bears (NFL)
1944 Chicago Bears (NFL)
1945 Chicago Bears (NFL)
Games: 23 (NFL)
1939, 1940,1941 AFL Champion
1943 NFL Western Division Title
1943 NFL Champion

A tackle fighting at Crosley Field, in the Xavier University Stadium or on the Corcoran Field, the three home-fields of Cincinnati. In 1939 Sigillo moves to the Bullies, the team which runs out of money before end-season and so accept to play also some roadgames outside the championship (and will later be considered the 1939 AFL champions). The reborn Bullies will be remembered for the great 1940 season (the best AFL record) and for the 1941 repeat. As a conclusion for these two seasons, the team of Sigillo will dispute some games against the champions of the Californian PCFL (*Pacific Coast Football League*): the so called *Championship of the small professional leagues.*

A few years later, a 230 pounds tackle gets to the NFL at the venerable age of 30. A lucky and winning debut, leading to an NFL title.

His name? Dom Sigillo.

JOSEPH S. «JOE» SIGNIAGO

OG-DG
Notre Dame
1948 New York Yankees (AAFC)
1949 New York Yankees (AAFC)
1950 New York Yanks (NFL)
Games: 26 (AAFC); 12 (NFL)

One of the many strong players of Notre Dame in the mid 40s (2 national titles in 3 seasons).

In the 1947 AAFC draft he is chosen in the 14th round by Cleveland; in 1948 he will make it to to sign a contract with the Yankees. Two years in the AAFC and an experience in the new NFL.

LEONARD «MEATBALL» «LEN» SIMONETTI

T
Tennessee
1947 Cleveland Browns (AAFC)
1948 Cleveland Browns (AAFC)
1947 AAFC West Division Title
1947 AAFC Champion
1948 AAFC West Division Title;
1948 AAFC Champion
Games: 38; Int. 1, 22 yards

A dominating tackle with the Tennessee Volunteers, among the college football Top 10 of 1946.

Len is put under contract by Paul Brown, who makes him a starter in the Cleveland team.

Simonetti (225 lbs.) is one of the 4 most «grown up» players of the Browns and in the course of his 2 seasons will know the satisfaction of winning 2 divisional titles and 2 titles of the league (1947: Cleveland Browns-New York Yankees 14–7; 1948: Cleveland Browns-Buffalo Bills 49–7).

ROCCO «ROCCI» SPADACCINI

B
Niagara
1941Columbus Bullies (AFL)
1948 Charlotte Clippers (AFL-Independent)
1949 Charlotte Clippers (AFL-Independent)
1941 AFL Champion

Together with the other Spadaccini (Vic) Rocco plays a good tournament; his team will win the title of the closing AFL (which will be back in a few years). In December 1941 Columbus will play against the PCFL champions Hollywood Bears in the game which will be defined *«the championship of the small professional leagues»*. 7 years later he is still on the track.

VIC SPINELLI

HB
?
1940 Newark Bears (AA)
1940 AA Playoffs

Another very small and faraway star quickly shooting through the pro sky at speedlight.

EDWARD A. «ED» STACCO

T
Colgate
1947 Detroit Lions (NFL)
1948 Washington Redskins (NFL)
Games: 14

The Lions giant (250–270 lbs.) arrives to the NFL in 1947; his will be a difficult experience, with meager satisfactions, lived at the bottom of the charts. The passage to Washington will give him a small-measure winning season (the Skins will rank 2nd in the Eastern with a 7–5–0 record).

ANTHONY E. «TONY» STALLONI

T
Delaware
None.
1946 Team Captain
1946 Mason-Dixon Conference MVP
1946 Tampa (FL) Cigar Bowl
1946 All-American
1946 Small College National Title
University of Delaware Football All-Time Team
University of Delaware Athletics Hall of Fame

He was a star at Delaware in the years 1940–1942 and in the 1946, after the military service.

3 important seasons culminating in 1946 with a record of 10–0–0, a winning streak of 31 games and a national title. The rocky lineman will play together with his 2 brothers (Mariano and Carl) and will be recognized as the best player of his conference. In 1947 he will be put under contract and then fired by the AAFC Baltimore Colts.

He will then become an assistant football coach in his own college (1947–1948) and later a salesman.

ALEXANDER J. STRUZZIERO

FB
Northeartern Univ.
None.
Northeastern University Hall of Fame

A small, dinamic fullback, a star of his college who sometimes kicks XPs, blocks in the offensive line and sacks in defense; in the spare time he is also a baseball star (captain of the team that in 1940 becomes champion of the New England) and a track protagonist (with great performances in the 100 and 600 yards). After the war, spent as a lieutenant in the Navy, he will begin a 28 years long career as the Massachusetts High School football officier.

SAMUEL J. JR. «SAM» TAMBURO

DE
Penn State
1949 New York Bulldogs (NFL)
Games: 12

One single season in the NFL with the unlucky team of Ted Collins, who has moved his franchise from Boston to New York. Despite the Polo Grounds (available when the Giants are away) and the *«circenses»* of the half-game break, the Bulldogs will never really take off, and at the end of the season the roster will be dismantled.

AMEDEO F. «ARMY» TOMAINI

T
Georgetown
1945 New York Giants (NFL)
Games: 8

He plays one single season as a pro and it is a singular moment, surrounded by the echoes of the war. The Giants end their season 3rd in the Eastern with a 3–6–1 record.

CARL A. TOMASELLO

DE-HB
Scranton
1940 New York Giants (NFL)
1941 Jersey City Giants (AA)
1942 Paterson Panthers (AA)

1946 Scranton Miners (AFL)
Games: 1(NFL)
Rec.: 21, yards 327, TDs 5 (AFL)
1941 AA Playoffs
1946 AFL All-League Team

After three good years in the college football team of Scranton, Tomasello plays his cards in the NFL.

One year as a Giants reserve, a 3rd place in the division. Then he moves for two years in the American Association.

In 1946 we find him back home in the AFL; in the farm club of the Pittsburgh Steelers he will realize 5 TDs

LOUIS V. «LOU» TOMASETTI

HB-DB-RB-WB
Bucknell
1939 Pittsburgh Pirates (NFL)
1940 Pittsburgh Steelers (NFL)
1941 Philadelphia Eagles(NFL)-Detroit Lions (NFL)
1942 Philadelphia Eagles (NFL)
Games: 41; Rush.: 178, 475 yards, TDs 2; Rec.: 19, 227 yards, TDs 2; Passing: 16–
53, TD 1, Int. 7; PRt: 6, 85 yards; KRt: 5, 108 yards

He arrives among the pros in a team that registers no positive notes. The following year he is still a starter and the Steelers (this is how they are renamed) start playing better; at the end of the season the owner Art Rooney will temporarily sell the franchise.

In 1941 Tomasetti lands to Philadelphia. After a quick passage by Detroit, he settles with the Eagles. He will never know a winning season.

ED TOSCANI

QB
Dayton
1949 Wilmington Clippers (AFL)

Yet another meteor in the AFL.

SALVATORE «SAL» TORTORA

HB
Ursinus
1941 Churchill Pros (AA-Independent)

Here is another paisà playing in the Churchill Pros, the team that harbors 14 former Steamrollers (among the others, Duke Abbruzzi, Ray Monaco, Frank DelMonico).

FELIX TRAPANI

G
LSU
None
1945 All-SEC Tea

One of the best guards of the whole SEC in the second half of the 40s.

FRANK J. TRIGILIO

RB-LB
Vermont
1946 Los Angeles Dons—Miami Seahawks (AAFC)
Games: 8; Rush.: 41, yards 126, TD 1

Trigilio signs with the Dons, where is also playing Angelo Bertelli, but leaves his small mark in the record book of Miami, the team he moves to in the course of the season. In Florida he is displayed in 4 games as a RB, highlighting himself as the second best player of the team behind Jimmy Nelson.

CHARLES L. «CHARLEY» TRIPPI

HB-E-DB-QB
Georgia
1947 Chicago Cardinals (NFL)
1948 Chicago Cardinals (NFL)
1949 Chicago Cardinals (NFL)
1950 Chicago Cardinals (NFL)
1951 Chicago Cardinals (NFL)
1952 Chicago Cardinals (NFL)
1953 Chicagi Cardinals (NFL)
1954 Chicago Cardinals (NFL)
1955 Chicago Cardinals (NFL)
Games: 99; Passing: 205–434, yards 2,547, TD Pass 16, Int. 31; Rushing: 687, yards 3,506, TDs 23; Rec.: 130, yards 1,321, TDs 11; PRt.: 63, yards 864, TDs 2; KRt.: 66, yards 1,467; Punts 196, yards 7,907; Int. 4, yards 93
1943 Rose Bowl MVP
1943 All-American
1943, 1944, 1945, 1947 College All-Stars
1946 Sugar Bowl
1946 All-Sec Team
1947 NFL Champion
1948 NFL Championship Game
1948, 1952, 1953 NFL All-Pros
All-Time Rose Bowl Team
All-Time Sugar Bowl Team
All-Time SEC Team
1940s All-Time College Football Team
1940s All-Pros Decade Team
COLLEGE HALL OF FAME
PRO FOOTBALL HALL OF FAME

The son of miner Joseph Trippi and housewife Jamie Attardo is born in Pittston (Pennsylvania) in the December of 1922.

He was a great, versatile player who imposed himself nationwide ever since his first college year. At Georgia he is a regular both in the football and in the baseball team: he will gain a long series of awards and in 1946 will be the major adversary of Glenn Davis in the rush for the Heisman Trophy. After being selected for many College Football All-Stars he receives the call from one of the most famous teams of the baseball Major League: the NY Yankees. Yet he will also receive the call as a first choice from the Chicago Cardinals, and he will be stolen from the diamonds of baseball and from the sirens of the AAFC thanks to the richest contract of the whole NFL.

In 1947 Trippi debuts as a pro and quickly confirms all his value, playing as a runner, receiver, quarterback and punt returner and gaining more than 1,100 yards; at the end of the season he takes part to the NFL Championship Game scoring 2 splendid TDs, the first after a 44 yards run and the second with a 75 yards punt return. The game, Chicago Cardinals-Philadelphia Eagles, ends 28–21. In 1949 he repeats himself: 2nd best runner of the league and second consecutive NFL Championship Game (payback of the Eagles: 7–0). In 1950 he suffers a bit the losing trend of the team; still he manages to write his name in all the main stats.

The following year Curly Lambeau (the famous former player and coach of the Green Bay Packers) is the coach of the Cards in clear crisis and decides to display Trippi mostly as a quarterback; Charley will play a great season, gaining 1,200 yards, adding 500 more in 78 carries, and scoring 4 TDs. In 1952 Trippi will score 4 more TDs covering all the main offensive roles; in 1953 a new head-coach uses him as a halfback and punt returner and Trippi ends the season as the best returner of the league. From 1954 on Charley will be mainly used in defense, where he will complete 3 intercepts; in 1955, aged 32, Tripp will transform into a full time difensive back, with only a few punts on the long distance.

At the end of a career in which he gained all in all more than 8,500 yards, Trippi will be the head-coach of the Cardinals for 5 years (1956–1957 and 1963–1965), filling the gap between 1958 and 1962 at the lead of the team of Georgia University.

AL TURRINZIANI

HB
Stanford
None

He is one of the runners of Stanford, taking part to th 1948 *Big Game*.

ENRICO R. «ROCKY» UGUCCIONI

E-DE
Murray State
1944 Brooklyn Tigers (NFL)
Games: 10; Rec.: 7, yards 94; PRt.: 1, yards 12, TD 1

Coming from the Connecticut, Uguccioni obtains a contract with the new Tigers, born from the Dodgers as a last attempt at remaining in the bridge borough. For Rocky and his teammates it will be a year to forget (0–10–0); at the end of the season the owner of the team will merge with the Boston Yanks.

SAMUEL FILADELFO «SAM» VACANTI

QB
Iowa, Purdue
1947 Chicago Rockets (AAFC)
1948 Chicago Rockets (AAFC)-Baltimore Colts (AAFC)
1949 Baltimore Colts (AAFC)
Games: 39; Pass.: 154–368, yards 2,338; TDs pass 18, Int. 32

He arrives to the AAFC in a team hinging on Angelo Bertelli, who suffers an injury very early and is out all the season. Vacanti finds himself in the lead with Al Dekdebrun. In 1948 the Rockets will start the championship with yet another owner and another coach (it is the third time in a row). This in the very moment when the AAFC Rockets share all the attention of the audiences with the Bears and the Cardinals playing in the NFL. In addition to this, the famous Elroy «Crazy Legs» Hirsch also reports a bad injury. Vacanti chooses to join the Baltimore Colts, where he will be the back-up of Y.A. Tittle for one single season.

GASPARE «VIC» VACCARO

QB
Florida
None
1949 North-South Shrine Game

He is the leader of Florida's offensive line between 1946 and 1948. At the end of the season he will be convoked for a Shrine Game.

IVO «IZ» VALLORANI

C
Upsala
1946 Newark Bombers (AFL)

An anonymous year for a center with good numbers.

FRED VENTURELLI

K
None
1948 Chicago Bears (NFL)
Games: 1; PAT 4–4, Points 4; FG 1–1, Points 3

A kicker out of the averages, neither small nor light, yet very heavy (235 lbs.) who is discovered at the age of 30 but will soon be abandoned by the «hound» George Halas. Venturelli did his part (7 points) but played only one game.

JOSEPH G. «LITTLE TOE» «JOE» VETRANO

HB-DB-K
Southern Miss.
1946 S. Francisco 49ers (AAFC)
1947 S. Francisco 49ers (AAFC)

1948 S.Francisco 49ers (AAFC)
1949 S.Francisco 49ers (AAFC)
Games: 54, playoffs 2; Rushing: 56, yards 201, TDs 2; Rec.: 5, yards 71; Int. 3; PATs 187–203; FGs 16–34; PRt.: 20, yards 237; KRt.: 9, yards 204; Total Points 253

Little Toe debuts in the second best franchise of the new league disputing 14 games in the double role of runner and kicker. The 49ers will rank behind the amazing Cleveland Browns. Vetrano leaves many marks in the team stats: running, receiving, scoring, kicking, returning, intercepting.

He will stay with San Francisco for 3 more years. The constants: he will always cover different roles (even if he will mainly serve as a precision kicker) and his team will always be 2nd behind the Browns. Also in the only AAFC Championship Game he will manage to play before the fusion with the NFL.

PAUL P. VINNOLA

HB-DB
Santa Clara
1946 Los Angeles Dons (AAFC)
Games : 13 ; Rush. : 23, yards 36; Rec.: 4, yards 39; PRt.: 2, yards 24; KRt.: 5, yards 83; Int.: 1, yards 41

In a single season he manages to leave a mark in the main stats of the Californian team. The life, anyhow, is elsewhere.

DON ZANGARA

T
Ohio State-Youngstown State
1949 Erie Vets (AFL-Independent)

One of the biggest players among the Vets with his 235 lbs.

JOSEPH «JOE» ZENO

G-T
Holy Cross
1942 Washington Redskins (NFL)
1943 Washington Redskins (NFL)
1944 Washington Redskins (NFL)
1946 Boston Yanks (NFL)
1947 Boston Yanks (NFL)
Games: 42; Int. 1
1942 NFL Eastern Division Title
1942 NFL Champion
1943 NFL Eastern Division Title
1943 NFL Championship Game

A succesful rookie who arrives to Washington, plays 9 games out of 11 and with his contribution allows the Skins to win the divisional title and to reach the NFL finals, won against the Chicago Bears. The story repeats itself in 1943, except for the results: the Bears take a heavy revenge. Uin 1946 Zeno signs with the Boston Yanks: his 240 lbs. make himè the secondo heaviest tackle of his team after Rocco Canale (256 pounds). In Boston he will play 13 games in 2 years.

LOUIS R. «LOU» ZONTINI

HB-LB-DB-K
Notre Dame
1940 Chicago Cardinals (NFL)
1941 Chicago Cardinals (NFL)
1944 Cleveland Rams (NFL)
1946 Buffalo Bisons (AAFC)
Games: 26; Rush.: 35, yards 97; Rec.: 4, yards 110, TD 1; Kick.: PAT 29–33; FG 5–15; Punts 14, yards 538; PRt.: 4, yards 47; KRt.: 3, yards 66; Points: 68

A nice experience with Notre Dame. In 1938 he is the protagonist of an 84-yards touchdown against the University of Minnesota: in the same year he is the second best runner of his college and one of the best blockers.

As a pro he plays 2 years with the Cardinals, 1 with the Rams (where he will devote himslef to punts and punt returns) and after one year in the Navy towards the end of the war, he also plays 1 year in the new league (he will score 42 points).

To be noted his participation to the movie *Knute Rockne, All-American.*

GEORGE ZOPPA

C
Cumberland
1948 Bethlehem Bulldogs-Newark Bears (AFL, AFL-Independent)
1949 Jersey City Giants (AFL)

Two complicated seasons in the AFL.

LOU ZUCCONI

C-T
Long Island Unv.
1941 Jersey City Giants (AA)

One season with the Giants that reach the playoffs only to be eliminated by the Long Island (final score: 6–7).

FRANK ZUZZIO

T-G
Muhlenberg
1940 Paterson Panthers (AA)
1941 Newark Bears (AA
1940 AA Playoffs

He played in the minor league first with the team led by Leo Katalinas and then with the farm club of the Bears led by Gene Ronzani.

978-0-595-47827-9
0-595-47827-1

Printed in the United Kingdom
by Lightning Source UK Ltd.
132488UK00001B/159/A

9 780595 478279